THE WAY OF A CHRISTIAN

LIFE LESSONS from PILGRIM'S PROGRESS

a 90-day
devotional

Chosen

a division of Baker Publishing Group
Minneapolis, Minnesota

© 2022 by Baker Publishing Group

Published by Chosen Books
11400 Hampshire Avenue South
Minneapolis, Minnesota 55438
www.chosenbooks.com

Chosen Books is a division of
Baker Publishing Group, Grand Rapids, Michigan

Printed in China

Library of Congress Cataloging-in-Publication Data
Names: Baker Publishing Group, other.
Title: The way of a Christian : life lessons from pilgrim's progress—a 90-day devotional.
Description: Minneapolis, Minnesota : Chosen Books, a division of Baker Publishing Group, 2022.
Identifiers: LCCN 2021043535 | ISBN 9780800762414 (cloth) | ISBN 9781493437160 (ebook)
Subjects: LCSH: Bunyan, John, 1628–1688.—Religion. | Bunyan, John, 1628–1688. Pilgrim's progress. | Jesus Christ—Devotional literature.
Classification: LCC PR3332 .W37 2022 | DDC 828/.407—dc23/eng/20211001
LC record available at https://lccn.loc.gov/2021043535

Written by David P. French

Cover design by Studio Gearbox
Interior design by Jane Klein

Baker Publishing Group publications use paper produced from sustainable forestry practices and post-consumer waste whenever possible.

22 23 24 25 26 27 28   7 6 5 4 3 2 1

Contents

Introduction

John Bunyan was born in Bedfordshire, England, in 1628. After his marriage, Bunyan accepted Christ and began to attend a church other than the Church of England. Subsequently, Bunyan became a nonconformist puritan preacher who was jailed for twelve years for refusing to stop preaching. During this period in jail, Bunyan started to write. His works included *The Pilgrim's Progress*, published as Part I in 1678 and Part II in 1684. *Pilgrim's Progress* is Bunyan's most enduring work out of 60 books and has been published around 1,500 times in over 200 languages, at times being second in popularity only to the Bible.

The Pilgrim's Progress deals by means of allegory with the Christian life. At the time of writing, it was not uncommon for the Church of England to persecute authors who wrote works that questioned some aspect of state religion. Writing by allegory became a way of protecting the author, as it put a wrap of mystery around what was being said, as well as being something akin to the parables of Jesus for inciting interest and debate.

Bunyan wanted to help the reader to discover the true path to heaven. So he was inspired to write his book as the dream of a traveler and describe his journey in terms of the difficulties and helps that he encountered along the way, which form valuable life lessons for Christian pilgrims following the same path.

In Part I, upon which this devotional focuses, Bunyan narrates the journey of Christian from the City of Destruction, where he first believed and realized his need to get out. After multiple trials, Christian and his companion traveler, Hopeful, finally reach the Celestial City.

The purpose of this 90-day devotional is to show the transcendent and eternal truths contained in Bunyan's story. Each day you will

- read a short excerpt from *The Pilgrim's Progress*, which is the inspiration for that day's devotional reading
- be enlightened and encouraged through a two-minute reading about how God helps us and how the enemy hinders us on our path toward our Celestial City
- reflect and apply what you have read to your life today
- connect with God through prayer about that day's theme

You may want to pair this devotional with a full reading of Part I of *The Pilgrim's Progress*. Or this devotional can stand alone as the excerpts help you recall key portions of this classic story. We trust this devotional will provide insight and faith to defeat the enemy, empower you to live a more victorious Christian life and bring you encouragement and joy on your pilgrim journey.

1 | A CHANGE OF CLOTHES

I saw a man clothed with rags.

Anyone who has not yet received Christ is spiritually destitute and clothed in rags. Other great religious leaders may have power to inspire the mind, but only Christ has the power to instantly transform an entire life and clothe it with righteousness.

At the beginning of his dream, and the story of *Pilgrim's Progress*, the dreamer sees himself as a poor man clothed in rags. It is a vision of his true spiritual state. The man clothed in rags is at a loss because he sees no hope, no way out, and only the certainty of God's impending judgment upon him and upon his city.

> For all of us have become like one who is unclean, and all our righteous deeds are like a filthy garment. —Isaiah 64:6 NASB

Not any amount of self-effort, or even a lifetime of sacrificial work on our part, could ever afford us cleansing such as Christ gives to anyone who in desperation and true repentance turns to Him. He washed us in His own precious blood to remove every stain and spot (see Revelation 1:5), and then He washed us again with His Word to remove every blemish and wrinkle (see Ephesians 5:27).

Our cleansing came at a great price, and so do the new clothes of salvation that we must keep clean by living holy lives so that we shall be unashamed at Christ's return (see Revelation 16:15).

The garments that we wear speak of our destiny and our priority. As the Bride of Christ, we are destined to be "married" to Christ. That marriage is also our greatest priority. When a bride is engaged to one whom she loves and wants to marry, she behaves prudently, as her desire is for their love to grow ever stronger in mutual trust and confidence.

- What spiritual clothes are you wearing today? Rags or righteous garments?
- How do your spiritual garments affect how you choose to behave?
- What do they say of your destiny?

Father, I thank You that I have been cleansed and clothed in new righteous garments ready for the wedding day. I praise You that these new garments speak of my new destiny. May I behave myself wisely while I live for You in this world and await the return of Christ.

2 | A CHANGE OF MIND

Christian no sooner leaves the World but meets Evangelist.

Great conflict often leads to a fight-or-flight response. In this century, hundreds of thousands have fled worn-torn countries or those ruled by despots. God sometimes allows us to feel disappointment, dissatisfaction, disillusionment or even despair in our lives to get us to turn away from the world we have known and go out in search of something deeper, more meaningful and longer lasting.

After coming under deep conviction, the pilgrim of *Pilgrim's Progress* tries to persuade his wife and children that they should all leave the City of Destruction. He knows his city is no longer safe and that it will soon come under God's judgment. The pilgrim knows that he needs to leave, but he needs someone to show him where to go. The pilgrim laments his pitiful condition with tears. Yet his wife and family consider him deranged, so in his disturbed state, he wanders about the fields, reading his book, until he meets Evangelist, who counsels him about what he should do; he begins a change of mind.

> For the sorrow that is according to the will of God produces a repentance without regret, leading to salvation, but the sorrow of the world produces death. —2 Corinthians 7:10 NASB

Repentance in its root sense simply means a change of mind leading to a change of behavior. It is when your changed mind begins to produce changed actions that God will send help to direct you further into a good path (see Matthew 3:7–8).

It is often only when one is somehow all alone that God can deal deeply with that individual (see Genesis 32:24). You may be reluctant to be first among your family or friends to follow Christ, but it is far better for you to set out on your own than to be forever lost.

- What do you know of deep inner conflict or disappointment?
- How might a change of perspective lead you to bold changes?
- How important are first steps when trusting God to show you a new way?

Dear Lord, I am tired of disappointment and inner conflict. I can never fight against Your will and win. Help me to begin to move away from areas where I should not stay and trust You to show me a new path and a better goal.

3 | A CHANGE OF DIRECTION

Do you see yonder wicket gate?

Have you ever gazed at the stars as a child, and someone pointed out a constellation to you? Perhaps they pointed somewhere and asked you, "Do you see the Great Bear?" You don't see it at all. But after much conversation you see what looks to you like a great bird from a comic strip!

In search of answers to the mysteries of life, including a search for God, you may want some unmistakable lights or grand signs to confirm the supernatural and your desire to be guided by such. But another human who has struggled as we have, has come to know a better way and can show it to us is exactly what we need (see Hebrews 4:15).

Christian meets Evangelist, another mortal man like himself. He could have been offended and thought, *The Almighty cannot be serious to send just a man when I need my own experience.* Evangelist asks Christian if he can see the small gate in the distance. He cannot. It is too far and too small, and he does not know exactly where to look.

But small is the gate and narrow the road that leads to life, and only a few find it. —Matthew 7:14 NIV

We sometimes find ourselves off track and need a change of course. We need someone who knows the way to point us in the right direction and tell us how to get there. We look for someone who appears to know where they are and what they are doing. The very person we need may have already recognized that we look lost. May our spiritual eyes be opened to discern a helper that the Lord has already put in place.

- Why do some people look for great signs before they can act?
- Whom may you have overlooked that God has sent to help you?
- What do you see that is a hopeful sign of change to come?

Father, where I have been guilty of seeking for signs rather than believing, forgive me. Where I have ignored or undervalued someone You have placed in my way to help me, forgive me. Help me to receive any guidance that You have sent, then reset and maintain a new course.

4 | A CHANGE OF FOCUS

Then said Evangelist, "Keep your eye firmly fixed on that light, and go directly up toward it; then you shall see the gate."

A grand master in chess is someone who looks at the same chess board and sees the same pieces differently. Experience of battles lost and won has taught her that the move that looks obvious to many must not be made, but the move that looks like a mistake could provoke checkmate in just three moves.

Christian is in need of someone who knows the next moves he must make along the way and how to recognize the right path. Evangelist is able to show him a shining light, and although to Christian it looks small and dim, Evangelist tells him not to take his eyes off that light until he arrives at the gate.

> Then Jesus again spoke to them, saying, "I am the Light of the world; the one who follows Me will not walk in the darkness, but will have the Light of life." —John 8:12 NASB

Have you ever been out on a pitch-black night walk with someone who is holding a light? You need to stay close to, or follow, the one holding the light, because he has light and without his light you would stumble in the darkness and fall.

We follow and stay on the path by fixing our eyes upon our great Savior and Mentor, Jesus (see Hebrews 12:2). As we habitually walk in His light, our own lives become transformed and filled with His light (see Luke 11:36). That simple change of focus and daily walking in the footsteps of the Master are what make those who follow Him closely the light of the world and will cause some in the world to give glory to God for our good works (see Matthew 5:14–16).

- How can you keep your eyes firmly and constantly fixed upon Jesus?
- How can you walk closely behind or beside Him (see 1 John 2:6)?
- In what ways can you chase darkness away so that others will glorify God?

Dear Lord, help me to fix my eyes on You so that Your light will flood my soul and transform my living. Teach me to walk in Your footsteps and always do good. May others give You glory because of the light that I bring by my actions.

5 | A CHANGE OF DESTINY

And, dying there, sooner or later, you will sink lower than the grave.

A fire alarm rings in a crowded office, and one senior manager decides it's false and stays put. The rest of the staff, seeing the manager looks unperturbed, believe he must have been told that there is no fire, so they stay inside and block their ears. Then suddenly there is an explosion and fire bursts across the entire open-plan office space. They all scream in terror, but it's too late! It shall be like that for those who ignore the warnings of God's impending judgment that will come upon an unrepentant world that refuses to heed His warnings and escape His wrath.

Christian has a clear vision of impending doom for the City of Destruction where he lives, so he flees. His wife, children and some of his neighbors seek to persuade him to stay, but he refuses to listen. He flees, seeking a change of destiny.

> But when he saw many of the Pharisees and Sadducees coming for baptism, he said to them, "You offspring of vipers, who warned you to flee from the wrath to come?" —Matthew 3:7 NASB

Just because we don't see a fire doesn't mean we should ignore the fire alarm. Neither does the absence of seeing impending judgment, or even God Himself, mean that we should ignore the clear warnings of Scripture.

The Bible teaches that we should each take responsibility for our own salvation. We cannot blame our parents or those who raised us, the government, some religious leader, a friend or lover. We shall each have to give a personal account for our own life before God (see 2 Corinthians 5:10; Hebrews 9:27). Let us take responsibility for ourselves and find out what we need to do to be saved (see Acts 16:30–31).

- Why do so many ignore God's warnings about impending judgment?
- What alarm bell is ringing in your life, and for what?
- How can you be sure to escape the destruction that is to come?

Father, help me never to stop my ears to Your warnings, but rather to heed them and take action. May nothing in this world be so sweet or convenient as to keep me from Your path. May I so live that my life will be precious in Your eyes.

"What!" said Obstinate, "and leave our friends and our comforts behind us?"

Christ demands that we be willing to lay down every relationship and every possession, if necessary, to follow Him wholly.

Christian has just left his own dear wife and children behind in order to escape. He knows that if he decides to stay that he will perish along with his city when the judgment comes. He tries his best to persuade his family, but they do not take him seriously. And Obstinate is not willing to forego his friends or his comforts.

> You cannot be my disciple, unless you love me more than you love your father and mother, your wife and children, and your brothers and sisters. You cannot come with me unless you love me more than you love your own life. —Luke 14:26 CEV

The demands of Christ are nonnegotiable! They are made on take-it-or-leave-it terms. With Christ, it is all or nothing. Once they realize what is being required of them, too many people either refuse to set out or else turn back partway.

The comforts of the world are many and varied. They center around selfishness. "I would rather do something else than gather to worship with other believers." "I would rather enjoy another vacation each year than give to that cause." "It's okay to have a few vices as long as they don't hurt others." "I hate trying to be nice to everybody."

But just as a chain-smoker with a cancer diagnosis must face hard and pressing choices, so must a pilgrim who would leave this world for a better one. One cannot keep an addiction or an unholy love relationship, or even a wedded relationship, if your partner now declares that unless you drop your faith your marriage is over. Christ must come first. Wherever He leads you, you must go.

- Why are some unwilling to leave worldly possessions for Christ?
- Why are some unwilling to leave other people for Christ?
- What does it mean to leave everything to follow Christ?

Father, help me in my weakness. It isn't easy to forsake all and follow Christ. Please teach me what it means to follow You completely and with my whole heart. Help me to love Christ more than any other person, yes, even more than my own life.

7 | A CHANGE OF HEART

I intend to go along with this good man.

An English proverb declares, "The road to hell is paved with good intentions." It is very bluntly making the point that merely wanting to arrive at the right outcome is not enough. You must both want it and be prepared to suffer in order to reach it.

Pliable is quickly and easily persuaded by Christian to journey with him away from the City of Destruction to a better life. Pliable has a change of heart for the better. Christian is glad to have a traveling companion. The two set off together in good conversation, looking for the little gate.

The apostle Paul used the illustration of a soldier to teach his spiritual son Timothy about the need for discipline along the way.

> Suffer hardship with me, as a good soldier of Christ Jesus.
> —2 Timothy 2:3 NASB

A soldier is someone under orders. The primary expectation of a soldier is one of unquestioning obedience. The two most commonly spoken words are probably "Yes, sir!" A soldier cannot reasonably respond to a command to march on with "But, sir, my feet are aching." A good soldier has a heart to obey orders.

If you have ever engaged in a truly long walk as soldiers do, you will know that there are many potential discouragements along the way. Poor footwear may cause blisters on your feet; poor clothing may leave you cold, wet, too hot, sunburned or frostbitten; inadequate food or drink may leave you wearied. To overcome these discouragements, you will need strong resolve, which may require a change of heart.

As good soldiers of Christ, we must build strong resolve and maintain it. We do so by the spiritual disciplines of Bible reading, prayer, worship, sharing our faith and, if we are able, fasting. Let us strengthen our changed hearts for the journey ahead.

- How can you respond positively to adversity?
- What can you do to ensure your intentions turn into positive actions?
- In what ways can you build and maintain your overall resolve?

Lord, make me a good soldier of Jesus Christ, the captain of Your army. Help me to obey His direction and not to complain or drag my feet. Show me how to clothe myself for all kinds of spiritual weather and adversity so that I can advance well.

8 | A CHANGE OF CONFIDENCE

And do you think that the words of your book are certainly true?

The truth of God's Word is central to the Christian faith. Those who don't believe or who doubt it will not be able to depend upon it. Only those who dare to trust God's Word fully will be able to prove its reliability. Unlike men, who often lie, God cannot and does not lie, so His promises can be entirely trusted.

Pliable first asks Christian if he knows the way. Then Christian refers to his book in order to satisfy Pliable's desire to know of the further things there are to be enjoyed when they reach Celestial City. This prompts a deeper question from Pliable as to whether Christian believes that the words of his book are true.

Every believer *believes*, by definition, but on what surety can we fix our belief?

> In the hope of eternal life, which God, who cannot lie, promised long ages ago. —Titus 1:2 NASB

The apostle Paul asserts that his hope is based upon the premise that God cannot lie. Paul reached this conclusion based upon (1) empirical external evidence and (2) internal personal experience.

You can do the same. You can check the truth of God by well over one hundred prophecies of the Old Testament that point to Christ. You can observe that so many of these have already been accurately fulfilled. For instance: Genesis 3:15; Psalm 22:15–18; Isaiah 53:3–6; all these pointed to the crucifixion of Christ hundreds of years beforehand.

Then from your own walk with the Lord, and learning to hear and listen to His voice, you will find that when He tells us, "Don't worry. I've got this," then the situation that looked impossible somehow works out just fine. God cannot lie.

- On what basis can you confidently trust in the Bible?
- How can you begin to hear the voice of the Lord?
- Why might your confidence that God cannot lie grow over time?

Father, grant me a confidence like that of the apostle Paul. Help me to study Your Word and confirm its reliability for myself. Help me to hear You clearly and believe what You say. May my trust in You and Your Word grow stronger and deeper with time.

9 | A CHANGE OF BAGGAGE

The name of the slough was Despond.

hristians are not immune from panic, helplessness, despondency, despair or depression.

Christian and Pliable have been speaking about the many wonderful and delightful pleasures that are before them at Celestial City. As soon as they finish talking, they inadvertently enter the Slough of Despond, and Christian begins to sink! Christian experiences this crisis because he is still carrying his load of sin to the cross. Christian does not fully understand where he is, what is happening, nor indeed what to do. Sin is an offense to God and exerts a load and a drag upon anyone who carries it.

> Cast your burden upon the LORD and He will sustain you; He will never allow the righteous to be shaken. —Psalm 55:22 NASB

Whenever we find that sin is causing us to sink, it should stir us to cry out to the Lord and cast our burden of sin upon Him. David, writing in Psalm 55 (as quoted above), had discovered a wonderful release from the load and drag of sin. He had learned that the Lord was so loving, that, if we would renounce our sin and cast the burden of it upon the Lord, then He would take hold of it and remove it from us completely (see Psalm 103:12). What a wonderful change of baggage!

When sin is not dealt with and guilt hangs over us like a thick dark cloud, it can create a sense of helplessness in us that may turn to despair. Despair can cause despondency, and lasting despondency can even lead to depression. Thank God that we can cast our burden of sin onto the Lord and receive His free pardon for the penitent (see Isaiah 55:7).

- How can consciousness of sin stir you into godly repentance?
- How can godly repentance cause you to cast your burden upon the Lord?
- How does casting your burden upon the Lord keep you from being shaken?

Dear Lord, stir my heart early in regard to any unconfessed or unforsaken sin. May I cast my burden of sin upon You and forsake every ungodly path. As I walk in Your ways, may You protect, preserve and shield me so that I am never shaken.

Then said he, "Give me your hand." So he gave him his hand, and he drew him out.

Perhaps you've watched an action movie that has a person hanging on to a treacherous ledge by his fingertips when a helper arrives and says in a firm voice, "Give me your hand!" We can see the danger of the person reaching out with one hand while he can barely hold on to the ledge with two. Yet we want the hanger-on to trust the voice, let go and grab that hand—knowing that unless that happens there can be no change for the better.

The character Help appears to Christian and lifts him out of the Slough of Despond, probes him with questions about his journey so far, answers his questions and then tells him many wonderful truths. Pilgrim stretches out his hand to Help when asked, and he receives a change for the better.

We all need help at different times in our lives. Sometimes we need more help than any human can give. But we have hope in God, for He will help us.

He brought me up out of the pit of destruction, out of the mud, and He set my feet on a rock, making my footsteps firm.
—Psalm 40:2 NASB

In this psalm David describes how God rescued him from a slippery pit of destruction, just as Help rescued Christian from the Slough of Despond. God wants to do this for you today. The greatest helper anyone can have is the Holy Spirit, whom Jesus said the Father will send (see John 14:26).

We all need to stretch out a hand in prayer in times of trouble and ask for help that may come from a human source, or from God Himself. Reach out to Him today and expect a change for the better.

- Where do you need God's help most?
- How is the Helper (the Holy Spirit) reaching out to you?
- What do you need to let go of to receive His help?

Lord, help me to know and trust Your voice. When You tell me to let go and hold Your hand, help me just to do it. Father, send the Helper in Jesus' name. If You send help by some other person, then help me to recognize it and trust the help You have provided.

11 | A CHANGE OF POLICY

He dwelt in the town of Carnal Policy, a very great town.

After buying insurance, your insurance certificate is accompanied by a policy document. The document determines the conditions upon which the insurance becomes activated, the extent of any potential payout and the exclusions. Each Christian needs to adhere to a policy in matters of morality that activates and pays more readily and at a higher level with less exclusions. In doing so we shall maintain a higher standard than the world, not to boast, but rather to maintain a good conscience and please our Lord. A Christian code of conduct, or policy, will often conflict with the policy of the world.

Mr. Worldly Wiseman, a leading citizen of the town called Carnal Policy, intercepts Christian along the way in the hope of diverting him away from the path to Celestial City. He has heard of Christian, whose departure from the City of Destruction had become a major talking point. Mr. Worldly Wiseman asks Christian a set of cunning questions designed to sow doubts in his mind about his recent change of policy.

Brothers and sisters, I could not address you as people who live by the Spirit but as people who are still worldly—mere infants in Christ. —1 Corinthians 3:1 NIV

In the early church at Corinth, the evidence of church people behaving no differently from the world was clear to the apostle Paul. He heard reports of immorality, and not just the more common incidents of marital infidelity or premarital sex, but of a man living with his stepmother (see 1 Corinthians 5:1). What most disturbed the apostle was not that they all knew about it, but rather that, knowing, they had not done anything about it. They had not enacted a change of policy.

- What areas of your life have practices that are worldly?
- How does your thinking need to change in order for your behavior to follow?
- How does growing in Christ lead to a more mature mindset?

Father, I don't want my life to blend in with the world. I am willing to embrace conflict where necessary in order not to compromise who I am and how I should therefore behave. Help me to grow in spiritual maturity and become more Christlike in my thinking, decisions, attitudes, habits and conduct.

12 | A CHANGE FOR THE WORSE

Christian turned out of his way to go to Mr. Legality's house for help; but when he reached up to the foot of the hill, it seemed so high.

H ave you ever tried to cut across a somewhat unfamiliar part of town on the hurried directions of a stranger to save time and ended up not knowing where you were? You felt sure it was going to work out well, but now you are in a tight spot because you have an important appointment to keep but time is about to run out on you.

Christian is persuaded by Mr. Worldly Wiseman to leave the narrow path and turn aside. He has been advised to take a look at the town of Carnal Policy with a view to calling for his wife and children to join him there. But as soon as he arrives, he can see that something doesn't look right.

> There is a way which seems right to a person, but its end is the way of death. —Proverbs 14:12 NASB

Rather than follow the same general way that the majority takes, a Christian must rub against the grain, turn into the wind and hold firmly to the narrow path that leads to life.

Those who don't understand our choice may laugh at us; they may try sincerely and with genuine good intention to have us turn back; but we must steadfastly resist and continue to move further away.

No number of generous acts of philanthropy can ever pay for our sins. If we find we have made a change for the worse, and find ourselves acting no differently from the world, then we need to stop, turn around and go back to the cross.

- How can you check your position to see if you have wandered off track?
- What might it cost you to keep moving in an opposite direction to the world?
- When might you need to turn around and go back to the cross of Christ?

Dear Lord, show me if my direction is right and if I am on track. Where I have strayed from Your ways, please turn me around and set me on a right course. Bring me back to the cross in repentance for forgiveness, cleansing and a new start.

13 | A CHANGE OF VALUES

For Master Worldly Wiseman can but show a saint the way to bondage and to woe.

F acebook began as a search for lost friends. Google is, at its core, a search for missing information. Instagram can show our world as we would like it to be. Twitter allows us to easily reinforce our worldviews. Yet what we are needing most is largely absent from these platforms. The greatest human need is an authentic walk with the Almighty.

Christian finds himself vulnerable to the attractive idea that there is an easy way to avoid the destruction that is coming and, subsequently, there is no need to leave his wife and children and endure the dangers, challenges and trials along the path to Celestial City. But when he heeds Mr. Worldly Wiseman's advice, and arrives near to Legality's home, he feels his burden grow far heavier and the sense of impending judgment grow strong, causing him to tremble and stop in his tracks, not knowing which way to go.

> The fear of man brings a snare, but one who trusts in the LORD will be protected. —Proverbs 29:25 NASB

Many in the world speak patronizingly to us somewhat along these lines: "For me life is all about home, family and close friends, so I am sure that any reasonable deity will see with me on that. I'm happy to take my chances."

It all sounds so reasonable. Yet it is lazy to the extent that the speaker has no urgency about seeking the truth and is either dishonest, or somewhat reckless, to the extent that there is no expressed discomfort about not knowing what the truth is, nor how embracing that truth might lead to a radical change of values.

- To what extent are you spending time in areas that cannot meet your greatest need?
- To what extent have you listened to "Mr. Worldly Wiseman" rather than God?
- What immediate action must you take to cause a change of values?

Father, forgive me for the hours I have spent searching for answers to my needs where they cannot be found. Help me to refocus my best time and attention wholly on You. May I reflect on what's most important and value my relationship and standing with You above everything.

He always goes to the town of Morality to church. . . .
It is his best way of avoiding the cross.

Good behavior is not enough to earn salvation. Man's reasoning about what is acceptable and sufficient for forgiveness and salvation does not align or reach up to God's.

If you engage in personal testimony with another and challenge that person to follow Jesus, you may hear the following kind of response: "Look, Mary next door goes to church and she's no better than me. So I figure I'll be all right when the time comes."

Christian has listened to Mr. Worldly Wiseman and for a short while believes that if he brings his family to the Town of Morality and attends church there with them, it will be sufficient to satisfy the demands of God. As Christian turns out of the good way, Evangelist meets him and is able to confront him, correct him and direct him back toward the narrow path.

They are from the world, therefore they speak as from the world, and the world listens to them. —1 John 4:5 NASB

To receive salvation as a free gift, you must first despair of your own righteousness, recognizing that it can never amount to the required standard (see Romans 3:23). You must accept that the penalty you deserve for such a lack of righteousness is death. Only then do you understand your true need for salvation as the free gift of God (see Romans 6:23). The change of standard you need comes as a free gift, accepted by faith, where Christ gives you His righteousness in exchange for your sin (see 2 Corinthians 5:21). Then you learn to walk in the power of the Spirit by grace alone (see Galatians 5:16; Romans 6:14).

- How could you avoid needing to be saved because you think you are good enough?
- How can you exclude worldly philosophies from your spiritual worldview?
- Why can you trust God for salvation and walk by grace alone?

Father, thank You that although I am not good enough, and never could be good enough for heaven in my own self, You have saved me by Your grace. Help me to trust in the righteousness of Christ alone and seek to walk daily in the power of the Holy Spirit.

Both he and those with him shoot arrows at those who come up to this gate, hoping to kill them before they can enter in.

The apostle Paul taught us that faith, hope and love all endure, but the greatest is love (see 1 Corinthians 13:13). Our tendency might be to discount faith and hope and focus on love. That would be like a painter saying, "My three greatest tools are my scraper, my brush and my roller, and my roller is the best; I'll put down my scraper and my brush and just use the roller!" It would be a poor change of tactics.

As Christian nears the wicket-gate alone, Goodwill the gatekeeper reaches out his hand and pulls him inside to protect him from the arrows of Beelzebub (another name for Satan) and his archers. Christian has not yet taken up his shield.

> In addition to all of these, hold up the shield of faith to stop the fiery arrows of the devil. —Ephesians 6:16 NLT

Three choice arrows that Satan uses are doubt about (1) what God said, (2) if it is true and (3) whether God really has our best interests at heart. In Eden, Satan first asked Eve, "Did God really say?"; second, Satan told Eve, "You will certainly not die"; third, Satan brazenly declared that God did not want her to eat that fruit and so become more like Himself (see Genesis 3:1–5).

We must learn a change of tactics that means holding the shield of faith against every dart that Satan shoots. If we have sinned, we should use our faith in God's mercies to quickly confess our sins and be forgiven (see 1 John 1:9) so that Satan cannot shoot at us with darts of guilt and shame.

- By what means should you take up the shield of faith?
- Why should you trust in God's Word, truthfulness and excellent intentions?
- How best can you clear up every sin with God?

Father, when I reflect on how Satan seeks to attack me in so many ways, help me to build myself up in Your Word and my knowledge of Your truthfulness and Your excellent intentions. Thank You for giving me the shield of faith that is effective against all Satan's fiery arrows.

We make no objections against any, notwithstanding all that they have done before they arrived here. They will never be cast out.

Whereas you say that somebody has "turned over a new leaf," it means that person has fundamentally changed in some way. That person has made a new beginning.

Christian is met at the wicket-gate by the gatekeeper Good-will, and on the other side of that gate is the narrow path leading to Celestial City. He has had doubts about whether he would be allowed to pass through at all, but he is warmly welcomed and is soon rejoicing that he is making a new start by taking his first few steps along the true pathway to life.

All that the Father gives Me will come to Me, and the one who comes to Me I will by no means cast out. —John 6:37 NKJV

There are countless millions who have yet to begin a new beginning with God. Christ has told us that He is not only the door of the sheep (see John 10:7, 9), but also the Way and the only way to the Father (see John 14:6). We come to salvation by coming to Jesus, and salvation cannot be found in any other name (see Acts 4:12). We see that the gate to life is indeed not wide, but it is very welcoming. Every weary traveler who turns sincerely to Jesus for salvation will find a big welcome and a new beginning.

For those of us who have experienced that new birth, the new beginning, we need to be conscious that we are wonderfully and undeservedly privileged. Today let us rejoice in the riches of our salvation and let us pray for opportunities to direct others about how to obtain them.

- When did you last turn over a new leaf in some area of your life?
- What is your experience of the warm welcome of Jesus?
- How can you help others to experience a new beginning in Christ?

Father, thank You that salvation is free and available to each one who sincerely turns to Christ. Thank You for the joy of Your salvation and the new beginning that comes with it. I pray for opportunities, wisdom and courage to share my faith today with others who don't yet know You.

17 | A NEW HOLINESS

Even as you saw the young girl lay the dust by sprinkling the floor with water, so is sin vanquished and subdued, and the soul made clean through the faith in the gospel.

Have you ever become so tired of a filthy environment that you rolled up your sleeves and did something to change it? There was once a traveling minister who stayed with a professional couple who were successful but disagreed about cleaning duties. As a result, their home became horrendously dirty over time, but it happened so gradually that they did not notice it. The minister waited until he could stand it no more, and then one day while they were at work, he vacuumed the messy carpets, cleaned out the refrigerator and removed layers of grease in the kitchen. The Holy Spirit acts like that visiting minister.

When Christian stops at Interpreter's house, he sees a man sweeping dust. The Interpreter explains that the dust is the Law, and the gospel is the water that lays down the dust and cleanses the room, thereby symbolizing the cleansing of a man's heart by the gospel. In this passage of *Pilgrim's Progress*, the Interpreter represents the Holy Spirit (see John 14:26),

. . . that He might sanctify and cleanse her with the washing of water by the word. —Ephesians 5:26 NKJV

The Holy Spirit lodges in the life of the believer. He is comfortable when the life of that believer is clean and peaceful. If we allow Him, the Holy Spirit will help to bring cleansing and peace. He brings cleansing by teaching us the truth and how to apply it, both from the Bible and from an inward witness (see 1 John 2:27). He gives us peace by assuring us of His presence in our lives (see John 14:27). Hallelujah! No more choking in a dusty room.

- In what ways has the Holy Spirit been speaking to you?
- What do you hear the Holy Spirt saying to you?
- How can your life remain cleansed, in order and at peace?

Father, thank You for the gift of the Holy Spirit, who is available to every believer. May I welcome the Holy Spirit in my life, and may I grant Him liberty to teach me how to hear and apply the Word to cleanse me and bring peace by His presence.

For first must give place to last, because last must have his time to come; but last gives place to nothing; for there is not another to succeed.

Those who by their passions urgently exhaust life's pleasures are satisfied first and scorn others who patiently wait for better to come. But for those who are patient, their time will come and the reward will not fade away.

Passion wants all the good things of the present life, and he laughs Patience, his companion, to scorn because he listens to the Governor, who has told them to wait a while for better things to come. Passion is the worldly one, the hedonist, who seeks to consume all that is here, believing there is nothing more, and it will soon pass. But Patience looks with eyes of faith into eternity, where what is to come will last forever.

> But Abraham said, "Son, remember that in your lifetime you received your good things, and likewise Lazarus evil things; but now he is comforted and you are tormented." —Luke 16:25 NKJV

Christ told a somewhat parallel story of an unnamed rich man who lived in great splendor every day, persistently ignoring the desperate plight of a beggar outside his own gates. Both men died, and the rich man went down to Hades (the waiting room for hell), and the poor beggar was carried to Abraham's breast. The poor man was comforted and in a position of high honor while the rich man was in a place of great suffering. Their life experiences had neatly reversed in the afterlife.

When the rich man cried to Abraham for help, there was none. Abraham knew how the rich man had behaved and that the judgment he received was well merited. A new age is coming when Christ reigns supreme. We are wise when we live for the age to come.

- How much are you like Passion and how much like Patience?
- How much are you investing in the life to come?
- What changes may be necessary in order to provide for eternity?

Father, help me to be more heavenly minded like Patience and less earthly minded like Passion. Help me not to be callous and lacking in compassion like the rich man Jesus spoke of. May I be led by Your Spirit to live modestly now and invest extravagantly for eternity.

And with that I saw many caught up and carried away into the clouds, but I was left behind.

Many Jewish rabbis teach their followers that the best day to repent most earnestly is the day before one's death. Since no one can be sure of when that day will be, however, the rabbis advise that the safest course of action is to repent every day.

Interpreter takes Christian to meet a man who has just had a vivid dream and has woken up trembling. The dreamer explains that, in his dream, Christ returned and commanded that the tares be tied up and burned and the wheat be gathered into His barn. But when Christ looked at him, he was convicted of his sins and knew that he would be left behind.

> Then we who are alive, who remain, will be caught up together with them in the clouds to meet the Lord in the air, and so we will always be with the Lord. —1 Thessalonians 4:17 NASB

We would be well advised to live in the light of Christ's imminent return at an unknown hour. Also, since none of us can be sure how long we will live, we would do well to clear our accounts with God on a daily basis (see Matthew 6:11–12).

The day one becomes a Christian by repenting from sin and accepting Christ as Lord and Savior is the same day one becomes a sharer in a new hope. This new hope is that one day the sins of this world will be judged, unrepentant sinners will be removed and we shall receive new bodies to live an everlasting life in a new heaven and earth. Let that precious hope motivate us to always go forward, no matter how hard the way.

- Why should you want to keep daily accounts with God?
- Can daily repentance and renewal help your prayers (see Matthew 6:15)?
- How much are you motivated by the Christian hope of an eternity with Christ?

Father, may I live my life with expectation of the imminent return of Christ. Help me not to store unforgiveness in my heart but to release those who have wronged me so I too may be forgiven. May I meditate much today upon the blessings that Christ's return will bring.

20 | A NEW LIFE

Blessed cross! Blessed tomb! Blessed rather be the Man who was put to shame there for me!

The divine exchange happens at the cross throughout eternity. In the mind of the Father, it happened before the foundation of the world. In the mind of the Son, it happened on the day of His crucifixion. In the mind of the Spirit, it happened at the hour the believer first believed. That divine exchange includes, first, our sin given, and His righteousness received; second, our sickness and infirmity given, and His health and strength received; third, our poverty given, and His riches received! That divine exchange gives us a new life.

Christian continues his journey following the directions of the Interpreter, and soon the path leads him up to a cross, where his burden loosens and falls from his back and into the tomb, where it forever disappears. Christian rejoices in the cross but even more in the Man of the cross, Christ.

> He made Him who knew no sin to be sin in our behalf, so that we might become the righteousness of God in Him. —2 Corinthians 5:21 NASB

When we see the cross of Christ and move toward it in faith, there is that divine exchange as our burdens become loosened, then removed and disposed of, and we receive forgiveness, cleansing and new clothes. Everything becomes new (see 2 Corinthians 5:17).

We need to be careful as believers not to rejoice in the gifts more than in the Giver. The Giver is always greater than the gifts, and while we are right to rejoice in sins forgiven, burdens and guilt removed, and a new life that is everlasting, we should mostly rejoice in the Father who was willing to send His only Son and the Savior who was willing to die in our place.

- What excites you about the divine exchange?
- How are the benefits of salvation, healing, deliverance and provision received?
- How can you celebrate the One who gave His all for you?

Father, thank You for being willing to send Jesus, who was willing to die on the cross in order that my sin, sickness and poverty would cross over to Him, and His righteousness and well-being and prosperity would cross over to me. I rejoice in these, yet more in You, the Giver.

Three Shining Ones came to him and saluted him with "Peace be unto you."

At the cross of Christ, the believer's sins that were like filthy rags (see Isaiah 64:6) are removed, and walking in a new life of righteousness brings us a new covering of righteousness, symbolized by white garments (see Revelation 3:18). Along our pilgrim journey, God's angels are sent to minister to us, the heirs of salvation (see Hebrews 1:14).

There are three Shining Ones who minister to Christian at the cross. The first declares his sins forgiven; the second strips him of his rags and gives him a change of clothes; the third puts a mark on his forehead and places a sealed scroll in his hand.

> And he responded and said to those who were standing before him, saying, "Remove the filthy garments from him." Again he said to him, "See, I have taken your guilt away from you and will clothe you with festive robes." —Zechariah 3:4 NASB

In this highly prophetic passage, Zechariah saw Joshua, the High Priest of his day, standing clothed in filthy rags before the Lord, and Satan opposed him. But the Angel of the Lord was by Joshua's side, and the Lord commanded that his filthy garments be removed and Satan be rebuked, since God had removed Joshua's guilt. Moreover, the Lord commanded that Joshua should be clothed in robes used for joyous religious festivals, with a clean headband fastened upon his head.

From millennia past, Zechariah painted a shadow of things that were yet to come for us as believers. The cross of Christ has removed the guilt of the believer (see Zechariah 3:9; Romans 8:30), the Lord will provide new robes of righteousness for every true believer (see Revelation 7:9), and His name will be written upon our foreheads (see Revelation 22:4).

- What is the ministry of God's angels toward true believers?
- When in your journey have you been conscious of ministering angels?
- How should our cleansing and clothing cause us to celebrate our faith more?

Father, I thank You that angels watch over my ways and minister to me in my pilgrim journey. I am so glad for the cross of Christ that has removed my guilt and shame. Cause me to rejoice in my new clothes and with a consciousness of Christ on my mind.

We were born in the land of Vain-glory and are going for praise to Mount Zion.

Instead of following the Way that God has provided to enter the Kingdom, the enemy wants us to think another way will get us there; he would rather lead us off track, where we will end up lost, confused, afraid and without any hope of salvation.

Christian meets Formalist and Hypocrisy, who have jumped a wall to reach the narrow path. These men have no spiritual rebirth. They suppose that any man can approach God to worship Him and be accepted. Formalist has an outward form of religion but not the Spirit. The gospel is in his head but not in his heart. Hypocrisy is as his name says.

> Truly, truly I say to you, the one who does not enter by the door into the fold of the sheep, but climbs up some other way, he is a thief and a robber. —John 10:1 NASB

The sheepfold is only properly entered through the door. Anyone trying to enter by another way has a wrong intention. Such a person wants something that does not properly belong to them. The sheepfold is where the protection and care of the shepherd is for the sheep. In the same way, the pathway leading to life is only for the righteous. Those who are not pure of heart and true worshipers of God will not remain on the narrow path.

Jesus spoke of the nations as being goats and sheep (see Matthew 25:32). The goats are the stubborn animals that rebel against His Word and do not do His will. Goats will leave the pasture and be happy wanderers. The sheep are those who listen to His Word and obey it.

- Do you believe Jesus is the only Way to the Father, or that there are other ways to receive the hope of salvation?
- How do those with a form of religion differ from those of true faith?
- In what way is Jesus the door? And what does the sheepfold signify?

Father, thank You that, although every human except Your Son Jesus was born in sin, each of us who has truly turned to Christ for salvation has been born again, entered the door and set out on the narrow way. May we never wander but press forward on the path to life.

They came to the foot of the Hill Difficulty;
at the bottom of which was a spring.

The Lord has so ordered our paths that, before a difficult and steep section of our pilgrimage, He has set a place of refreshing so that we may be strengthened before we set out to climb.

Christian, with Formality and Hypocrisy following a little way behind, comes to the spring. Formality and Hypocrisy each take separate ways around the hill that leads to Danger and Destruction, but Christian gladly refreshes himself before beginning the difficult climb.

> They will not hunger or thirst, nor will the scorching heat or sun strike them down; for He who has compassion on them will lead them, and He will guide them to springs of water.
> —Isaiah 49:10 NASB

The children of Israel were scattered by God after the rebellion against Rome and the subsequent destruction of Jerusalem in AD 70. Yet God prophesied through Isaiah that even if a mother could forget her children, God would never forget His people (see Isaiah 49:15), but would bring them back, refreshing them along the way (see verse above).

Isaiah prophesied that a King shall reign in righteousness, and He will be as a hiding place from the wind and a shelter from the storm, "like streams of water in the desert and the shadow of a great rock in a parched land" (Isaiah 32:1–2 NLT).

No wonder that Jesus calls us to come to Him and find rest (see Matthew 11:28), and that if we are thirsty, we should come to Him and we can drink until rivers of living water begin to flow from inside of us (see John 7:37–38). Let us refresh ourselves daily for what lies ahead.

- How can you refresh yourself before a big challenge?
- What is something practical you can do to find shelter in Christ?
- Why do the rivers of living water from Christ never run dry?

Father, thank You for making provision for my journey every day. I thank You that my thirst and coming to Christ are what cause the rivers of living water to spring up inside of me. May I drink deeply today, so that being refreshed, I may also refresh others.

Mistrust and Timorous ran down the hill,
and Christian went on his way.

Traveling the narrow path all the way to heaven is not a journey for the fainthearted. We may be weak, doubting, even fearful at times, yet our love for Christ must overcome every fear.

At the top of the Hill Difficulty, Christian is met by fearful Timorous and doubting Mistrust, both of whom, upon considering how things seem to only get harder, have turned around and are hurrying back the other way. Christian reasons that he would face far worse going back than if he pressed on, so he gathers up his courage and presses forward.

There is no fear in love, but perfect love drives out fear, because fear involves punishment, and the one who fears is not perfected in love. —1 John 4:18 NASB

An old-time preacher would tell new believers, "All you need is a made-up mind." That preacher was not full-time, had never been to seminary and could not even read. Yet when he began to minister what the Spirit of God brought to his remembrance from the Word, the hair of many younger would-be preachers would stand on end as the presence and fear of God filled the place.

A new courage comes upon a believer whenever a new resolve has set in, empowered by the Holy Spirit. The believer looks at the same seemingly impossible, impassable or overwhelming situation, but with eyes of faith, and says, like Queen Esther, that even if I perish, I shall go where I need to go (see Esther 4:16). May God grant us such eyes of faith and such a bold resolve.

God told Moses that the people had walked around this mountain for far too long. It was time to head somewhere (see Deuteronomy 2:3). And what of you, today, dear reader, is it time for a new courage in your life?

- What causes a believer to become fainthearted?
- Why did the children of Israel spend years wandering in circles?
- What is the Holy Spirit's role to provide supernatural resolve and courage?

Dear Lord, help me to have a made-up mind, that no matter what, I am going to press forward with You, and that there will be no turning back. Thank You, Holy Spirit, for Your presence, direction and a new courage to move forward overcoming all obstacles.

Keep in the center of the path, and no harm shall come to you.

For a Christian, to be in God's perfect will is to be in the safest place. It may be the fire that Daniel's three companions were thrown into; or the raging Sea of Galilee, where the disciples were tossed in fear; or the place where Stephen was stoned. But with Christ beside us in the fire or the vessel, we shall pass safely through the storm, whether we remain on earth or move into His presence.

Arriving at the palace Beautiful, Christian sees two lions there, and because of the dark he is unable to see that they are chained, there merely to test the courage of pilgrims. Fortunately, the porter, Watchful, sees him before he turns back and tells him how to proceed safely at the center of the path.

> For whoever wants to save his life will lose it, but whoever loses his life for My sake and the gospel's will save it. —Mark 8:35 NASB

Our Lord requires courage on our part. It may not be natural to us in our simple human state, but courage is an integral part of our new nature in Christ that we need to discover. Imagine the new courage that the three young Hebrews discovered when they were thrown into the fiery furnace, met there by One like the Son of Man, and reemerged with their bindings removed and not a single hair of their heads singed (see Daniel 3:24–27).

Just like these three Hebrews, we should see our storm, trial, sickness, infirmity or other pressing need as something that can enable us to meet Jesus in a new way and inject supernatural courage into our personal faith.

- Why might I be hesitant for God to reveal His will for me?
- How can I be sure of what God's particular will for me is?
- What is likely to change if I should fully surrender to and pursue God's will?

Father, forgive me of any hesitancy in regard to Your particular will for me. Help me to trust in Your good intentions and ability to discern what is the ultimate best for my life. In my situation reveal Your will. Grant me grace to fully surrender and pursue Your will.

Fear of God's judgment can be the initial motivation to turn to Christ and seek salvation. But only when the Holy Spirit empowers us with new vision to see the desperate condition we are in, apart from God, can we be so moved. We must pray earnestly that God will remove every blockage from our eyes, hearts and minds and also from all those with whom we would share the gospel.

Christian explains to Piety how it was a vision of his own imminent destruction in the City of Destruction, where he resided in his native country, that led him to simply get out of there in search of a safer place.

> Whoever strives to save his life will lose it, and whoever loses his life will keep it. —Luke 17:33 NASB

Christ gives a paradoxical instruction in the above verse. He declares that if a man seeks to preserve his life, then he will lose it. Yet a man who doesn't want to preserve his life would be considered mentally unbalanced. By "strives to save his life," Christ was speaking of the selfish desire to keep things as they are because no change is desired by that person. Christ is declaring that only a wholesale discontent with preserving one's life—a discontent that demands something better, no matter what the price—will allow a person to become saved.

The change God desires is not primarily one of outward circumstances; that may come consequentially. No, God desires an inward transformation that will affect the whole person, just as leaven (a living yeast-based mix) works unseen inside a batch of flour to produce dough (see Matthew 13:33). It will bring a new paradigm that affects our entire worldview.

- What have you seen in your world that has brought you to the point of despair?
- In what ways has God brought inward transformation to your life and vision?
- How can inward transformation bring changes to how you see your daily life?

Father, thank You for rescuing me from Your judgment that is coming upon this world. Open my eyes to see a new pathway to life. Help me to not be happy with a worldly life but to be inwardly transformed until my entire vision and life are affected for good.

Prudence inquired, "Do you not sometimes think of the country that you left?"

Looking at the past is a temptation for any pilgrim. But it can be a distraction and hindrance to finding the narrow path that lies ahead. There is great joy and motivation that can come when we choose to fix our hearts on the final destination of heaven.

During their discourse at the palace Beautiful, Prudence is testing how fixed in his own mind Christian's commitment to the pilgrim journey is. She knows that without a mind that is set on Zion, a pilgrim may easily turn back. Christian assures her that he is only set upon going forward. Each of us should be similarly persuaded.

> But as it is, they desire a better country, that is, a heavenly one. Therefore God is not ashamed to be called their God; for He has prepared a city for them. —Hebrews 11:16 NASB

Our thoughts are the greatest determinants of our inward happiness. Consider a poor beggar who has never known government assistance or medical aid, nor has any roof over his head; yet he thanks God for the kindness of others, and for the sunshine that warms his tired bones. But most of all he contemplates sweetly that, one day, he will go to be with God.

Meanwhile a rich lady wonders why, if God is so loving, does arthritis cause an aching in her fingers at least once a week. She is constantly annoyed that her husband has told her she should wait until next year to get a new car, and she is even more annoyed with those preachers who speak of how sweet heaven will be.

Today, let us be those who find reasons to be happy about life, and especially if we are in Christ, and so eventually headed to that eternal heavenly home.

- How positive is your thinking in general?
- How satisfied are you with your life?
- How focused are you on your final destination?

Father, in Proverbs 23:7 Your Word teaches us that a man is as he thinks in his heart. May my heart think good and positive thoughts and find many more reasons to be thankful than to be discontented. May I look beyond this life to where Your saints will dwell forever.

Charity said to Christian, "But you should have talked to them, and have endeavored to have shown them the danger of being behind."

From the days of Lot in the time of Abraham, society has often scorned warnings about the impending wrath of God, yet the duty of God's people to warn and to intercede for sinners remains.

Nineveh was a city that immediately heeded God's warning sent by the prophet Jonah, whom they had never seen or heard of before (see Jonah 3:6–10). Christ proclaimed that wicked Nineveh was surely more righteous than the generation He warned and prayed for, yet they did not repent (see Matthew 12:41; 23:37).

Charity tells Christian that he ought to have severely warned his family of the impending destruction that would come upon them. Christian protests that he did, but that they would not take him seriously.

So Lot went out and spoke to his sons-in-law, who were to marry his daughters, and said, "Up, get out of this place, for the LORD is destroying the city." But he appeared to his sons-in-law to be joking. —Genesis 19:14 NASB

Sadly, Lot's attempt to save the two men engaged to be married to his daughters fell on deaf ears. Lot, his wife and his two daughters fled from the destruction, but the two men perished with the rest of the populations of Sodom and Gomorrah when these cities were destroyed by burning sulfur from heaven (see Genesis 19:24). Their salvation was a direct result of Abraham's pleading with God (see Genesis 18:32).

In the face of possible ridicule, our duty to continually remind men of these truths, and their need to repent, remains pressing, and indeed is something that we cannot escape (see Ezekiel 33:6).

- Why do people often fail to respond to the warnings God sends?
- What are some obstacles you face when talking to others about matters of faith?
- What is the best possible outcome for those you have warned and prayed for?

Father, thank You for the Bible, which gives us the story of Jonah, who at first resisted Your call to go to Nineveh and preach. May You help me overcome any reluctance, fear or indifference on my part to share my faith and pray for others, to see some saved.

They showed him first the pedigree of the Lord of the hill,
that he was the son of the Ancient of Days, and came
by that eternal generation.

The praise, honor and worth of our Lord and Savior ought to be the first matter we discuss when we meet with other Christians along the way. Often our conversational priorities can be centered on lesser topics of no real eternal significance.

Piety, Prudence and Charity sit down with Christian for a long talk about his journey so far. They examine why he came without his family and those he encountered along the way, and his experience at the cross. Then they talk at length about the Lord of the Hill.

> He is the one whom God exalted to His right hand as a Prince and a Savior, to grant repentance to Israel, and forgiveness of sins. —Acts 5:31 NASB

Our thinking is a reliable litmus test of our true spirituality. We may think much about good things yet lack true spirituality. For instance, we may think constantly about our children's education, our business, the safety of our neighborhood, or even the poor, but without including much thought of our Lord and Savior, our spirituality is lacking in depth.

The reason making the Lord a big part of our thinking is so important is that He is truly unique and above among men, among spiritual leaders and throughout time. He is the preeminent One; long before Abraham (see John 8:58), He was there as the Word through whom the world was created (see John 1:1–3). His is the only name in whom salvation may be found (see Acts 4:12). Christ is our perfect example, and our priority in serving Him must come first (see Luke 14:26).

- Why is it easier to think about matters on earth rather than about Lord Jesus?
- How can thinking and speaking much about Jesus help you?
- Where do you want to direct your primary attention today as you do your work?

Father, help me to think much and speak much about Your Son, Jesus. Help me not to force Him on anybody who is not interested, but lead me by Your Spirit to find others who love to speak of Him and those who are wanting to know more about Him.

It is a hard matter for a man to go down into the Valley of Humiliation, as you are about to, and not to slip and fall in the process.

Some people don't like being talked well of; they say it embarrasses them. But anyone who enjoys humiliation is considered abnormal. Humiliation can come about by a variety of means. One is by association, and it is amazing how quickly some "friends" will distance themselves from someone who has fallen from grace, and this only adds to their humiliation.

Prudence forewarns Christian that no man enjoys going into the Valley of Humiliation. Yet it is a necessary part of the pathway that the Lord has set in order for a Christian to reach the Celestial City. Prudence warns Christian that he might slip, and he does. Yet he gets back up and continues in his journey, as must we.

Humble yourselves, therefore, under God's mighty hand, that he may lift you up in due time. —1 Peter 5:6 NIV

The Bible declares that the just shall fall seven times, meaning that such will fall completely, but then they will get up again (see Proverbs 24:16). Peter personally denied Christ three times in his time of greatest need (see Matthew 26:75). Yet once Peter had been restored, he loved Christ more, depended upon him more and feared to trust in his own strength.

Paul begged the Lord for a "thorn in the flesh" to be taken away, and the Lord denied his prayer three times, replying that His grace is made perfect in weakness (see 2 Corinthians 12:8–9). No matter what it is that takes us into a valley of humiliation, let us stay there long enough so that when God graciously leads us out, we shall walk afterward more in His strength and less in our own.

- When have you experienced the Valley of Humiliation?
- How much has social media made humiliation more likely and painful?
- How should we respond when we, or friends of ours, fall and are humiliated?

Father, help me to be a friend to those who are being humiliated, knowing that one day I may need friends to stand with me through a time of humiliation. Help me to humble myself during any period of humiliation and not emerge from it until I can rise again in Your power.

Apollyon raged, "I am an enemy to this Prince; I hate his person, his laws, and people; I am come out on purpose to withstand thee."

We may easily forget that we have an unseen enemy. Many believe Satan to be as much a fiction as Santa Claus, but they are gravely mistaken. In addition to being conscious of Satan's existence, we should seek to become even more aware of how he wages war against the believer.

Christian first meets Apollyon with his eyes, and he is an ugly and fearsome sight. Then as Apollyon approaches, Christian determines to stand his ground. After much dialogue, Christian is not persuaded by Apollyon's slippery deception or false promises.

We need to be aware of Satan's means and methods to deceive us, defeat us or destroy us so that we are not caught off guard.

> So that no advantage would be taken of us by Satan, for we are not ignorant of his schemes. —2 Corinthians 2:11 NASB

The apostle Paul had many encounters, suffered much resistance and fought many battles with Satan (see 1 Corinthians

15:32). Before his conversion, Paul (then called Saul) had been deceived by Satan into believing he was doing the right thing in persecuting Christians (see 1 Timothy 1:13). After his conversion, he often faced opposition from the same Jews with whom he had worked before (see Acts 17:5), as well as fresh opposition on many occasions from those who were idol worshipers (see Acts 19:25–26).

Paul had also learned that the battles he fought with Satan began in the flesh, ascended to the mind and finally moved into the spirit realm. You need to know that, with the help of the Holy Spirit and by employing spiritual weapons, you will surely overcome (see 2 Corinthians 10:4).

- Why might you tend to forget that you have an unseen enemy?
- Where has Satan been attacking you recently?
- How can you overcome where Satan is pressing you the hardest?

Father, while I would always rather think of You, may I not forget that I have an enemy, Satan. Make me a wise and prepared soldier who always puts on the armor You give me, and, being on guard, I shall resist Satan, so that he shall flee from me.

Christian nimbly stretched out his hand for his sword and caught it.

A Christian must never give up, no matter how pressed upon or seemingly defeated. The battle is not over as long as there remains the will to fight.

Once Christian and Apollyon's lengthy and increasingly tense discussion becomes exhausted, with neither side willing to give way, Apollyon reveals his true ugly character, angry emotions and deadly mission. There follows a monstrous and dangerous battle that tests Christian's faith and resolve to the limit. Christian is about to be killed when he somehow reaches his fallen sword and, striking a fierce blow, badly wounds Apollyon, causing him to take flight.

Do not rejoice over me, enemy of mine. Though I fall I will rise; though I live in darkness, the Lord is a light for me. —Micah 7:8 NASB

One of the key determinants of lasting success is the ability to bounce back after a loss, fall or failure. Several of the largest and most innovative companies in the world actively recruit people who have previously failed big in the area they will be responsible for. God has an even longer track record of recruiting those who have failed big. When we fail, we ought to take time to reflect on what went wrong and determine how we will do better going forward. The very fact that we have come back to try again shows that we have the resolve needed to move past temporary failure to longer-term success.

Unlike Christ, His followers know what personal failure feels like, and we need to know that if we repent sincerely, then we will be forgiven and restored to good standing with the Lord (see 1 John 1:9). Then standing in God's grace, filled with faith and His Spirit, we overcome our adversary, Satan.

- What schemes and plots of Satan against believers do you presently see?
- Why can you as a believer live free from a fear of Satan?
- How should you best respond if you should suffer a temporary defeat?

Father, in regard to my enemy Satan: Open my spiritual eyes to understand his crafty and deceitful ways; help me to put on heavenly armor and fight whenever he contends against me; should my feet slip help me to repent, gather my resolve and then fight until he flees.

WHATEVER HAPPENS

> *Now, at the end of this valley was another, called the Valley of the Shadow of Death, and Christian needed to pass through it.*

S atan is not the only unseen enemy that we face. The apostle Paul taught that our battle in life is never against other human persons, but rather against the forces behind them that are spiritual in nature (see Ephesians 6:12). Whatever happens, we must press on.

We must pray for our eyes to be opened so that we will see that the forces of God with us far outnumber any opposing forces aligned with Satan (see 2 Kings 6:17). We must also fear God more than any other being, and be willing to face even death, declaring that whatever happens we will not bow or turn back (see Daniel 3:18).

Christian moves from the Valley of Humiliation into the Valley of the Shadow of Death, where the tests are worse than his battle with Apollyon. He is immediately met by two men fleeing back out from where he is headed, declaring that the dangers ahead are too much for a man to face. Yet Christian decides that whatever happens, he has to continue.

They did not say, "Where is the LORD who brought us up out of the land of Egypt, who led us through the wilderness, through a land of deserts and of pits, through a land of drought and of deep darkness, through a land that no one crossed and where no person lived?" —Jeremiah 2:6 NASB

Jeremiah lamented that God's people had so quickly forgotten their God who had delivered them from slavery in Egypt and led them through an uninhabited and dangerous wilderness and sustained them there. His point was that whatever happens, God is unfazed and more than able to deliver.

- What is a "Valley of the Shadow of Death" that you have passed through or need to pass through?
- What victories has God already given you?
- How can you move forward in some way today?

Father, thank You that You have both me and Your enemies surrounded. Thank You for the past victories of salvation, deliverance and healing that You have brought about in my life. May I meditate upon these things and determine and declare that, whatever happens, I will never turn back.

By and by the day broke.

An old English proverb asserts that "the night is never so dark as just before the breaking of day." The point of the proverb is that when things seem at their darkest, we should maintain hope, because in just a little while, things may never seem so bright.

Indeed, it turns out to be so in some ways for Christian, who is battling through the hardest part of his journey so far, with countless dangers on every side. And then at last the dawn finally breaks. In the brightness of daybreak, the path ahead shows itself even more dangerous, but with the advantage of seeing clearly, it can be navigated safely.

> He who made the Pleiades and Orion, and changes deep darkness into morning. —Amos 5:8 NASB

Many believers have known long nights due to some burden or pain. Their "night" may be in worries about a family member, or a matter of life and death, or overwhelming financial or business matters. Sleep evades them, but if they will just hold on and cry out to God, then the morning star will arise in their hearts (see 2 Peter 1:19).

A ship caught on a dark night by a raging storm in a tempestuous sea is alarmed, yet helped when a sailor spots a lighthouse. Before sight of it, the captain was unsure of where land was and unaware of the dangerous rocks the lighthouse warned them of.

The breaking of day brings clarity. What was lurking in the shadows—which we saw as some dreadful threat—may in the brightness of daylight turn out to be something we can use to our immediate advantage. Let us endure the night knowing there shall be such brightness and clarity when the new day breaks.

- What is the burden that you want God to relieve?
- How did day finally break after a dark night you experienced?
- How might God's light turn your perceived problem into a blessing?

Father, when the night is darkest, help me to remember that You spoke and commanded, "Let there be light!" and it was so. By that same power and word may light break forth into my every darkness, bringing clarity and purity and allowing me to clearly see the way forward.

Christian cried again, "Slow down, wait till I catch up to you!"
But Faithful answered, "No, my life is at stake because
the avenger of blood is behind me."

An ambulance driver on an emergency call employs a flashing light and a siren to warn other traffic that the mission is urgent. The speed of an ambulance can be a matter of life and death.

When Christian first sees his old neighbor, Faithful, on the narrow path, he is slightly ahead and higher up. Christian calls to Faithful to stop or slow down, but he will not, replying that he is running for his life. Faithful has a very clear sense of his greatest priority, the urgency of it and the danger of slowing down or stopping.

> Then she saddled the donkey and said to her servant, "Drive the donkey and go on; do not slow down the pace for me unless I tell you." —2 Kings 4:24 NASB

In this passage of Scripture, the Shunammite woman Elisha stayed with had an emergency and hurried toward the man of God. Her first priority was to get help for her dead son, and she was willing to push her donkey and her servant to move quickly.

Things that are important to us but have a deadline in the future, such as filing tax returns or choosing a new school or college, often get left well alone until the deadline looms close, and then a new urgency takes hold. What can be more important than securing our eternal salvation? Some leave going about it until they sense death is imminent. Let us not be so careless; rather, let us make haste to find the way of the Lord and to walk in it.

- How do you distinguish between the urgent and the important?
- What can you learn from Faithful and his unwillingness to slow down?
- What are you willing to push in order to pursue what is both important and urgent?

Father, thank You for the example of Faithful, who shows such a clear sense of priority and urgency in his pressing on. May I learn from him and become more zealous in my pursuit of what is both important and urgent. May I push aside all that distracts or slows me down.

I met with one whose name was Wanton, who would have liked to have misbehaved badly with me.

Fleshly desires are one of Satan's chief temptations used to pull a Christian off the path of the righteous. The youngest Christians may not know them yet; for the older ones, the temptations may be fading or past; but for a majority, and therefore quite probably for you, this is a present battleground. The pleasures of the flesh are sweet and short-lived and can cause permanent spiritual loss.

Faithful relates to Christian how he passed through various perils along the way, including an adulteress called Wanton. She flattered him and enticed him to indulge in immorality with her. Faithful managed to escape by shutting his eyes, but if he had not resisted, he would have been brought low.

Her feet go down to death; her steps lead straight to the grave.
—Proverbs 5:5 NIV

In this passage Solomon warns his own children about the dangers of an adulteress. Solomon was no prude and was an illegitimate child who wrote the love book of the Bible, Song of Solomon, yet he also knew the dangers of adultery and the value of fidelity.

The apostle Paul recommended marriage as a way to resist sexual temptation (see 1 Corinthians 7:2, 9). But he also taught that sexual temptation is simply a form of greed that is itself a form of idolatry, because, by placing our own will above that of the true God, we value man above God Himself. Paul taught that the way for you to overcome sexual temptation is by being more grateful for what the Lord has already given you (see Ephesians 5:3–5).

- How can you have apparent spiritual stature but be brought low by the flesh?
- How will considering long-term consequences help you in resisting the flesh?
- Why by regularly giving thanks will you be able to combat greed?

Father, may I resist fleshly temptation that I shall not be brought low by it. Help me to consider what giving in would do to my reputation, my family, my friends, my church and others who may look up to me. Help me to be truly grateful for all I already have.

He said that he had just three daughters: The Lust of the Flesh, The Lust of the Eyes, and The Pride of Life, and that I should marry them all if I would.

Worldly companions will be happy as long as you behave in much the same way as they do. That means indulging your appetites—whether for food or anything else you like the look of, or for making yourself seem better than others. Uncontrolled appetites are contrary to what God desires for us.

At the bottom of the Hill Difficulty, Faithful tells Christian, he met Adam the First, who said that he lived in the town of Deceit, and that if Faithful should choose to come and live with him, he could marry all three of his daughters and become his heir. Faithful was about to go when he observed a warning on the man's forehead and realized it was a trap.

For everything in the world—the lust of the flesh, the lust of the eyes, and the pride of life—comes not from the Father but from the world. —1 John 2:16 NIV

Make no mistake, the world has plenty to offer, but it has no lasting virtue, brings no lasting reward and comes with great personal danger. That's why the Bible warns us that the very form or fabric of this world is passing away, or transitory (see 1 Corinthians 7:31).

Children may naively build sandcastles on the beach and expect them to still be there the next day. Christ warned us to not be like the foolish man and build houses on the sand (see Matthew 7:26). Stop building sandcastles. Build for eternity. Set your spiritual eyes on the unseen realm and walk by faith and not by sight (see 2 Corinthians 5:7). The world is a distraction.

- What is the likely reaction of outsiders if you determine to live fully for Christ?
- Why would it have been a mistake for Faithful to take up Adam's offer?
- How can you avoid being distracted and keep Your focus on spiritual matters?

Father, help me to accept the likely loss of worldly friends in order to have a closer walk with You. Please warn me if I am being distracted so that I will avoid being led into temptation and danger. Grant me clear spiritual sight so that I can follow the right path.

*That man who overtook you was Moses. He spares no one,
neither does he know how to show mercy to those who
break his law.*

How sweet it can seem to speak from a place of moral
superiority over the failings of others. Yet how bitter
it can be to be on the receiving end of such pronouncements.
As we mature, we ought to recognize, as the apostle Paul did,
that there is nothing intrinsically good in us at all (see Romans
7:18) except the work of the Holy Spirit, and therefore what
we are greatly in need of is mercy.

Faithful relates how he climbed up the Hill Difficulty,
passing the shady resting place where Christian had
dropped his scroll. Then he was overtaken by a man who
struck him down and beat him mercilessly, almost killing him.
He was rescued only by the direct intervention of the One
(Christ). Later, Faithful realizes that the man beating him was
Moses, whom he had met before in the City of Destruction.

Anyone who has ignored the Law of Moses is put to death
without mercy on the testimony of two or three witnesses.
—Hebrews 10:28 NASB

Jesus warned His followers not to be swift judges of others, explaining that, later at the judgment, our own standards that we applied to judging others will be turned around and applied to judge us (see Matthew 7:1–2). Christ also taught us that it is a blessing to be a merciful person, as those who are givers of mercy shall also become recipients of it (see Matthew 5:7).

We each have ample opportunity to show mercy, should someone annoy us at work, at the checkout, at the bus stop, driving along the highway, or in any number of ways.

- Why was Moses unable to show any mercy at all (see Galatians 2:16)?
- What long-term benefits will you accrue by being merciful?
- Who needs your and God's mercy today?

Father, thank You that I am no longer under the law but rather under Your grace and mercy. Help me to see the wisdom of being someone who loves to show mercy to others. Open my heart to receive more of Your lovingkindness so that I may freely share it with others today.

Let us continue to resist him; for notwithstanding
all his bluster, what he promotes is foolishness.

S hame seeks to deceive us. Shame tells us it is a shame
not to enjoy the benefits of a little dishonesty, or to have
a tender conscience that makes a man less manly, or to risk
everything following Christian principles. But the final consequence of ungodly behavior—the guilt, the cowardice, the
foolishness and the very shame itself—will all be shame!

Faithful continues recounting his journey so far and speaks
of Shame, who he said would be more aptly named Shameless.
Shame objected to belief in God, a tender conscience, honesty
and any questioning of science. Faithful was unable to answer
Shame until he came to the realization that only God's values
and will, and the consequences of such, would ultimately prevail.

The wise inherit honor, but fools get only shame. —Proverbs
3:35 NIV

Jesus taught that wisdom is justified by all "her children,"
meaning all she produces and those who depend upon her
(see Luke 7:35). Every action has consequences, and those

consequences render a verdict as to whether the action taken has proved wise or foolish. If we let shame inhibit us from making the right choices—whether they be moral, spiritual or those of principle—the ultimate consequence would be of us incurring lasting shame.

We need to remember that the eyes of the Lord are constantly watching us (see Proverbs 15:3). He is weighing our thoughts and intentions by His Word (see Hebrews 4:12), so He is able to rightly judge whether we acted from a fear of shame or a fear of God. Let us look to the finish line and run this race in good conscience, banishing shame. May the consequence of our courageous and righteous choices be the commendation of our service by Christ.

- When was the last time you recognized the fruit of shame in your life?
- How was Faithful finally able to shake off his fear of shame?
- Where do you need to keep your focus to receive Christ's commendation?

Father, help me to resist giving in to the fear of worldly shame at the expense of not making the right choices. Thank You for awakening my conscience to Your truth. Grant me grace and courage so that I may follow You wholly, until one day I receive the commendation of Christ Himself.

Talkative . . . is the very stain, reproach, and shame of religion to all that know him; there is barely one good word spoken of our faith in that entire area of the town where he lives.

What you are speaks more loudly than what you say. A fervent person may go out evangelizing widely and speaking with apparent conviction and boldness. Yet if this herald of truth has not been inwardly changed by personal experience of the new birth, then his or her proclamation comes only through head knowledge. Others may be brought soundly into the Kingdom while the herald that helped them with the gospel shall be cast out! What vanity!

When Faithful first sees Talkative, he is ahead and walking in the same direction, but to one side. He says he is on his way to the heavenly country, and he would love to enjoy profitable conversation with Faithful along the way about every kind of spiritual matter. Faithful then excitedly tells Christian about him. Christian is unimpressed, as he already knows very well that Talkative's ability to speak like a zealous believer is nothing more than vanity.

As it is written: "God's name is blasphemed among the Gentiles because of you." —Romans 2:24 NIV

Parents and teachers are in a position of setting behavioral standards for those under their care. They will not be respected by the children they instruct unless they exemplify the behaviors they call for, such as respect, tolerance, patience, politeness, truthfulness and timeliness. Christians are role models to all those outside our faith. If we do not do as we say, then outsiders will lose respect for us. May God help us to match good talk with a good walk lest our professed faith be nothing more than vanity.

- How does what you talk about reflect on who others think you are?
- What inward transformation have you experienced in your own life?
- How can you best keep your walk in-line with your talk?

Father, may what I do right speak more loudly than the weaknesses I exhibit so that my words will not be contradicted by my poor behavior. May my testimony of spiritual matters come mostly from my own personal experience rather than from any head knowledge or teachings of others.

Indeed, to know the right thing pleases talkers and boasters, but to do it is what pleases God.

Politicians, car salesmen, real estate agents and criminal con men are all often thought of as being people who are untrustworthy. They often say the right thing to gain influence while in their hearts and lifestyles they practice something contrary. As those who profess Christ, we must ensure that our actions match with our claimed beliefs: first, so that we please God; and second, so that we do not bring shame to the name of Christ. This requires practiced learning of obedience.

Having warned Faithful that Talkative talks a good talk but doesn't walk a good walk, Christian then counsels Faithful to press Talkative in regard to whether and how he practices the things he so clearly approves of. This would challenge Talkative to either own up to his hypocrisy and receive abundant pardon (see Isaiah 55:7) or leave their company. Not long into this new conversation, Talkative leaves them, as he is unwilling to repent and obey God.

> Give me understanding so that I may keep your law and obey it with all of my heart. —Psalm 119:34 NIV

Psalm 119 deals with God's Word. The Bible is by far the most read and studied book on our planet. Yet while God is pleased for His Word to be distributed so widely, how much is it understood, or even more, how much do people who read it put it into practice? The psalmist here has grasped the need for proper understanding as a prelude to obedience.

May the Lord help us to understand in order that we can obey, because only obedience to His Word pleases God, not mere understanding of it.

- Why do so many talk a better talk than the walk they walk?
- How does an understanding of God's Word open up your willingness to obey it?
- How can your actions give a better reflection of your understanding of God's will?

Father, help me to be more than just someone whose only saintliness is in their words. Help me to understand why Your Word commands doing some things and not doing others, and then help me to obey Your Word fully so that I may please You in my daily actions.

42 | WHAT A HARVEST

I have sowed, and you have reaped.

Many Christians are daunted at the prospect of sharing their faith publicly or even privately. Fear of a less than positive, derisory or hostile response acts as a deterrent. But for those who obey the leading of the Spirit, when He prompts them to speak, there is promise of great and lasting reward.

As the two pilgrims, Christian and Faithful, are almost out of the wilderness, Evangelist comes and joins them. Evangelist had sown the seed of the gospel, and it found good ground in their hearts. When Evangelist the sower and his two converts, the reapers, meet again much further along the narrow path, they all rejoice together at the progress attained since they last met.

> Already the one who reaps is receiving wages and is gathering fruit for eternal life, so that the one who sows and the one who reaps may rejoice together. —John 4:36 NASB

Christ encouraged His disciples to take a look over into the fields because they were ripe for harvest. He was not speaking of the physical crops but of the hearts and souls of men that could be planted with the seed of the gospel and an immediate and miraculous growth would cause them to become instantly made ready for harvest.

We need to ask the Lord to open our eyes to see what He sees. Too often we see what looks like a hostile world that doesn't want to listen. But the Holy Spirit is able to pinpoint specific people around us who are crying out on the inside for someone to talk to them about the meaning and purpose of life and the deeper truths that will set them free.

- What barriers keep you from sharing the gospel?
- When Jesus looks at those around you, what do you think He sees?
- Who is the Holy Spirit highlighting who has an earnest desire to know God?

Father, grant me boldness, grace and wisdom to share the gospel of Jesus Christ with others. May I reflect deeply on the joy of those who have shared their testimony with others. Open my eyes and show me who I can share my faith with, especially somebody close to me.

Here are to be seen, too, and without any charge, thefts, murders, adulteries, false swearers, and each of a full-blooded kind!

The Western world loves to be entertained. We enjoy a laugh, a drama, suspense, intrigue, murder mysteries, action movies, musicals, plays, romance and so much more. Endless hours are spent on social media sites, apps and streaming services. While Christians might engage in such, we must be very careful that such distractions are not allowed to crowd out our devotion to and service of our Lord.

For countless millennia, pilgrims have followed the narrow path to the Celestial City. Three sworn enemies of pilgrim travelers and the Lord they serve—Beelzebub, Apollyon and Legion—conspired to build Vanity Fair across the path in order to distract pilgrims and congregate villains to oppress and abuse them. But Evangelist now warns the pilgrims of what to expect and that they will need to be prepared to withstand the opposition.

> Therefore, as a witness of the Lord, I insist on this: that you no longer walk in the outsiders' ways—with minds devoted to worthless pursuits. —Ephesians 4:17 VOICE

There may not be a huge theme park or some massive entertainment venue nearby where you spend your day, but the distractions of a modern vanity fair are rarely far away. Today all you need is a smartphone and a social media application, and you can easily spend half your day in relative idleness.

The apostle Paul gives a warning to the Ephesian church not to have their minds filled with worthless pursuits. We need to invest in our own spiritual growth and development in order that we can serve our Lord by serving others. Let us heed this biblical warning and watch how we use our days.

- How can you enjoy entertainment and remain on God's narrow path?
- What is one major distraction that threatens the use of your profitable time?
- In what ways are you deliberately feeding your spiritual growth and development?

Father, help me to heed the warning not to be like those who don't know You. Help me to develop an awareness of the things that threaten to distract me and waste my time. Allow me to develop positive disciplines that will strengthen me to serve You and others better.

44 | WHAT WILL YOU BUY?

"What will you buy?" But they, looking gravely upon him, answered, "We buy the truth."

We have a myriad of choices for how we can invest valuable resources such as time, talent and finances. But what will produce the greatest yield for our godly good?

Christian and Faithful arrive at the town of Vanity Fair, where they are beset by sellers of various goods. Sensing no interest from Christian and Faithful, and simply to have a dig at these strangers who irritate them by being so different, the merchants ask, "What will you buy?"

This is a question asked of believers. A colleague, neighbor or relative wants you to attend an event or participate in an activity that pricks your conscience. But you are serious in your walk with Jesus, and these people conclude from your response, with some obvious irritation, that you are no fun!

Our consumerist world provides an endless catalog of possible goods and services to buy. In contrast, truth is a commodity that seems in increasingly short supply as humankind prefers a watered-down or counterfeit version.

> Buy truth, and do not sell wisdom, and instruction, and understanding. —Proverbs 23:23 DRA

The Holy Spirit helps us discern that the value of the truth is far beyond and far more enduring than all the wares and vanities of this passing world. More of God's pure and perfect truth means more of Christ.

Jesus once told a parable of a "merchant on the lookout for choice pearls. When he discovered a pearl of great value, he sold everything he owned and bought it" (Matthew 13:45–46 NLT). Jesus is that priceless pearl. He *is* truth, and His value outshines all the world has to offer.

- What is the world influencing you to "buy"?
- If your treasure is where your heart is, then where is your heart?
- What are you willing to forfeit to obtain more of Him?

Father, I do not want to be a consumer or hoarder of things, but rather a seeker of Christ and one willing to spend much to have more of Him. May the passing glories of this earth grow dim, and the light of Your face shine brightly in my life.

45 | WHAT CONFLICT

Envy said, "I heard him once myself affirm that Christianity and the customs of our town of Vanity were diametrically opposite and could not be reconciled."

There will always be a conflict between desires for worldly satisfaction and desires for the things that satisfy God. For example, many want the pleasures of intimate relationships without the restrictions and responsibilities that God requires. This difference in views produces great conflict between Christians and those outside our faith.

Christian and Faithful endeavor to avoid the extensive array of things, people and pleasures for sale in Vanity Fair. Even though they speak the language of Canaan, which the men of Vanity Fair cannot understand, they are falsely accused of bringing disturbance to the town and its trade and are locked up in a cage. Evangelist had forewarned them of what conflict they would face.

> For the flesh desires what is contrary to the Spirit, and the Spirit what is contrary to the flesh. They are in conflict with each other, so that you are not to do whatever you want.
> —Galatians 5:17 NIV

The fact that our inner being desires something does not make it right. If we were to allow our children unlimited sweets and unlimited time playing games or watching films, then we are likely to witness them experiencing health problems and poor academic achievement. God will not allow His children to follow their desires when they become unprofitable, but He will bring discipline (see Proverbs 3:12) that will cause us to recognize the conflict (see Hebrews 12:11).

God does not discipline us because He is a killjoy, but rather because He wants us to have fullness of joy. Let us therefore learn to submit to the leading of the Holy Spirit so that our inner conflict is kept low.

- What conflicts between right and wrong are you aware of in your own life?
- When were you last aware of the discipline of the Lord?
- How has God's discipline helped to bring you toward greater maturity?

Father, the tension between what I want and what is best for me may always be there. Thank You for the times when You bring loving correction. Help me to see things more from Your perspective and less through worldly eyes so that my life will experience less conflict.

46 | A BETTER TESTIMONY

Superstition said, "I heard him say that our faith was worthless, and it could never please God."

As Christians, we may be asked to give an opinion on certain matters that are presently controversial. Over centuries and even millennia, there has been an ongoing conflict, since the values of our world and its rulers, both the seen and unseen, are in direct opposition to those of our Lord (see Ephesians 6:12).

After Christian and Faithful encounter harsh persecution in the town of Vanity Fair, Faithful is brought before a judge, Lord Hate-good. Various witnesses have brought evidence based on their conversations with him or what they have heard him say. Superstition is the second witness, and he testifies that Faithful denounced their faith as being of no value since it is wholly incapable of pleasing God. All this is true, but sadly, no better testimony of it can be given.

We have found this man to be a troublemaker. —Acts 24:5 NIV

During the first century AD, the accusation of being a troublemaker who stirred up trouble in the city had been leveled at Paul, who had faced the accusation square on with a denial that infuriated his accusers, who sought his immediate death (see Acts 21–22). His testimony was of better things, but they were unable to hear it.

In the final analysis, we are advised to live at peace with all men wherever possible (see Romans 12:18). But Paul, the writer of this counsel, knew from firsthand experience that to maintain a better testimony, this keeping of the peace would not always be possible. We remain in this same dilemma in our day. While we can sometimes choose to say nothing, there may be occasions when our conscience demands we find courage and give a better testimony.

- What can you remember saying in defense of truth that caused controversy?
- What spiritual forces lie behind the opposition of many to hearing the truth?
- Why should we sometimes be willing to sacrifice peace for truth to be heard?

Father, forgive me for those times when I kept silent, but not from wisdom or good conscience, but because the fear of men exceeded my righteous fear of You. Give me courage when what You lead me to say is controversial, and help me to season words of truth with Your grace.

Pickthank said, "I have known of him a long time and have heard him speak things that ought not to be spoke."

In the Western world we have strongly defended freedom of speech. More recently there have been restrictions imposed by governments in many countries to outlaw remarks that are deemed hateful or racist. A Western court can now judge you by your speech. In many other countries such freedoms have never existed, and a wrong remark against a powerful leader could provoke the harshest of responses. What better report ought Christians to give?

Before Judge Hate-good, and standing trial for his very life, Faithful is accused of saying things that ought never to have been said. Specifically, he is accused of speaking unjustified and libelous words against most of the "noblemen" of Vanity Fair. While Faithful had indeed spoken against them, he said nothing untrue, for they were the kind of men about whom one could give no better report.

> Blessed are you when people insult you and persecute you, and falsely say all kinds of evil against you because of Me.
> —Matthew 5:11 NASB

On the contrary, the reports given about many faithful Christians before their accusers have been patently untrue. Yet our words remain a yardstick by which others assess us, and even the Lord will use them in judging us (see Matthew 12:37).

What is needed is for our spoken beliefs and our practical actions and lifestyle to match up. In the end what we say will only carry weight if it is exemplified in the way we conduct ourselves. May we strive to hear that better report from Christ declaring, "Well done, good and faithful servant!" (Matthew 25:21 NIV).

- What is something you would like to say yet feel constrained not to say?
- How aware are you of Christians who are being persecuted for their faith?
- What are you doing to ensure that your words and your actions line up?

Father, help me to work within the confines and constraints of the laws of my land and not to bring trouble on myself unnecessarily. May the words of my mouth be pleasing to You, and my acts align with Your will for my life so that I shall joyfully receive Your commendation and reward at the end of my pilgrimage.

*Lord Hate-good concluded, "For the treason he has confessed,
he deserves to die."*

There are people who have silenced their conscience by rejecting its counsel (see 1 Timothy 4:2). They prefer dishonest gain and the company of other corrupt persons (see Ezekiel 22:27). They so hate those who are honest that, if it is in their power, they will sentence them to death rather than have some dead conscience pricked back to life (see Acts 7:57). They acutely lack that sense of a better belonging that is a distinctive hallmark of those who truly know and love God.

Judge Hate-good's hatred of honest Faithful is made clear at the end of the three testimonies. He shouts at Faithful, declaring him to be a renegade, heretic and traitor. He grudgingly allows Faithful to speak a few words in his own defense. It is clear the belonging of the judge and jury is to a far lower and darker sort of master and dwelling than that better belonging of Faithful to Christ and heaven.

> If you belonged to the world, it would love you as its own. As it is, you do not belong to the world, but I have chosen you out of the world. That is why the world hates you. —John 15:19 NIV

During the English Reformation in the sixteenth century, there were great tensions and conflicts between the Catholic Church and the emerging Protestant Church (which became the Church of England) and later between the Church of England and the emerging forms of "free" Protestant churches, firstly the Puritans and later the Calvinists. Men chose to put doctrinal differences above the greater principles of God's law, those of love and mercy. In their fanaticism toward their particular brand of doctrine, they often persecuted those whose true faith gave them deep assurance of a higher and better belonging.

- Where is your primary sense of belonging? With men or with God?
- Why have professing Christians sometimes persecuted each other?
- How can a sense of ultimate belonging help a Christian endure suffering?

Father, help me to know that, ultimately, I belong to You, and that Christ has gone to prepare an eternal dwelling place for me. May I not place my loyalty to some earthly belonging above that of my heavenly belonging. May I operate by love, the royal law of heaven.

The first among them, Mr. Blind-man, the foreman, said,
"I see clearly that this man is a heretic."

Governments are tempted to use their considerable pow-ers to influence the appearance of what seems to be true. They may seek to influence appointments to the highest courts. They might seek to appoint someone of apparent stature who they believe they can steer to become the chair of an "indepen-dent" inquiry or commission. They could hire expensive con-sultants and "independent" experts who they believe will tend toward the conclusions or recommendations they would like. In line for a probable loss of standing or a huge cost of making good, governments are tempted to avoid a better truth.

Judge Hate-good sums up the proceedings for the benefit of the jury before declaring his need to direct them toward finding Faithful, the accused, guilty. The foreman, Mr. Blind-man, makes a statement that directly contradicts his name, declaring that he can clearly see the guilt of Faithful! Each of the other jurors displays his own prejudice in bringing condemnation upon Faithful. The judge and each member of the jury are strangers to a better truth.

All who make idols are nothing, and the things they treasure are worthless. Those who would speak up for them are blind; they are ignorant, to their own shame. —Isaiah 44:9 NIV

No idol is truly divine. The prophet Isaiah exposed idols for what they were—worthless. The idol could not think, know, hear, see or speak for itself. Yet some foolish ones worshiped these idols. They lacked knowledge of the true God. They lacked a better truth.

When we know and follow Jesus as the Messiah, the Anointed One, the Christ, the Son of the Living God, the Lord and Savior of all who truly repent and trust Him, then we become those who have been enlightened with a better truth.

- Why does promoting a lesser truth tend to end in shame?
- How can bias or prejudice that is not dealt with cause us to miss the truth?
- What is the better truth that true Christians possess?

Father, may I be prepared to own up or apologize, when necessary, rather than to cover up. May I resist the temptation to misdirect others when the truth is uncomfortable or costly. May I buy truth so that I can know what is right and remain in good standing before You.

50 | A BETTER END

Thus came Faithful to his end.

Every believer must learn that work for God is only truly accomplished by His grace enabling our resolve to serve Him. Many Christians want the life of blessings but forget that our Lord suffered much and called us to take up our cross and follow Him. We would do well to strengthen ourselves in the Lord with the disciplines of sacrifice, self-control, prayer, study and fasting. Then, should a critical test of faith ever present itself, we will have the courage to do well by refusing to deny Christ, and make it to a better end.

Following strong direction from Judge Hate-good, the jury of miscreants find Faithful guilty, and the judge sentences him to death of the cruelest kind imaginable. Yet in heaven, the blood of Christ, Faithful's testimony and his love of Christ will speak for him more than the words of all those who spoke against him on earth. It will be a better end in eternity than what his cruel enemies see of it in this world.

And they overcame him because of the blood of the Lamb and because of the word of their testimony, and they did

not love their life even when faced with death. —Revelation
12:11 NASB

The apostle John saw that the saints of God overcame Satan by three means. First, faith in the blood of the Lamb, meaning that they had believed in the price their Savior had paid in love for their redemption. Second, the profession and demonstration of the word of their testimony of Christ living within them and through them. Last, their passion for their Master, whom they had determined to serve wholeheartedly and truly even at the cost of their very lives. These three means led them to a better end.

- What disciplines can we use to strengthen ourselves in the Lord?
- What is the expected end of those who reject the Lordship of Jesus?
- What three means gave victory to the faithful martyrs that John saw?

Father, I want to be faithful till my end—no matter what it is. Help me to practice prayer and be devoted to Your Word and the leading of the Holy Spirit so that my feet are planted upon the Rock and I walk in paths of righteousness for Your name's sake—even in the face of opposition.

51 | A BETTER HOPE

As one died for bearing testimony to the truth, another arises out of his ashes to be a companion with Christian in his pilgrimage.

The Bible records others observing the behavior and confidence of God's people or hearing the report of His dealings with His people, and seeking to share in their hope. Lot joined with Abraham, Rahab joined with the sons of Israel, Ruth joined with Naomi, and Lydia joined with the apostle Paul. Each connected with a better hope.

After Faithful is martyred, Christian undergoes a period of imprisonment before he is released and allowed to leave Vanity Fair. He is accompanied on his journey to Celestial City by Hopeful. Hopeful assures Christian that many others have been persuaded by the witness of the pilgrims and will follow in his steps. Hopeful has found a better hope.

> When they had driven him out of the city, they began stoning him; and the witnesses laid aside their cloaks at the feet of a young man named Saul. —Acts 7:58 NASB

Saul (later named Paul) was a witness to the death of the first Christian martyr, Stephen. Saul witnessed firsthand the confidence and courage of Stephen in the face of death. Later at the end of his own Christian journey, when he faced death and was executed in Rome, Paul would undoubtedly have drawn on the better hope that he first saw in Stephen.

The Christian life is not always easy, and for some it is difficult from the very outset. Yet what gives us courage and strength to persevere is the hope that we have in Christ. Hope that springs out of having our sins forgiven and entering into everlasting life—hope of an eternity with Christ and the blessed saints throughout the ages. It is a better hope.

- Whose behavior, confidence or testimony has inspired you?
- What hope do you see today that will help you in your present adversity?
- In what ways is the Christian hope a better hope than that of the world?

Father, thank You for those who have given me strength by their good example, faith and testimony. As I reflect on what they have imparted to me, may I rejoice as I consider the better hope I have, and earnestly pray for those who don't know You or Your love.

When religion is wearing his silver slippers, we so love to walk with him in the street, especially when the sun shines and the people applaud him.

There are societies and times in which Christians are generally well thought of, and others in which they are not. When Christians are well thought of, it is easy to profess our faith to others. When Christians are not well thought of, they are left with the purest of motives, the desire to please God. That singleness of heart leads to a better profession.

Along the way, Christian and Hopeful meet By-ends, who is from a town called Fair-speech. By-ends wants to keep company with the pilgrims, but neither they nor he are able to reconcile two differences. First, By-ends would rather do nothing than strive against prevailing trends. Second, By-ends would gladly pursue religion so long as it could be done with plenty, ease and acclaim, but not if it would lead to poverty, personal discomfort or a lack of recognition by others.

> Pure and undefiled religion in the sight of our God and Father is this: to visit orphans and widows in their distress, and to keep oneself unstained by the world. —James 1:27 NASB

The apostle James was a straight talker, and he declared that proper practice of the Christian faith involved ministering practically to those most in need. To James, professing faith without good deeds was a dead profession.

In the Church today, it can be easy to care more about how the building looks and how high definition our broadcasts are than whether we are meeting needs in our local communities. But what matters most is not the appearance of the building or broadcast; rather, it is the extent that a church is able to practically demonstrate Christ's heart for a hurting world.

- How much prosperity, good times or recognition motivates your faith?
- How closely do you walk with other professed Christians whose views differ?
- What are the purest motives one can have for helping the needy?

Father, search my heart and show me whether my motives for serving You are pure or if they are tainted. Cause me to follow You more closely with a pure heart full of love for You and others. Give me Your heart of compassion for orphans, widows and others in need of Your compassion and care.

Mr. Hold-the-world added, "I can only consider him a fool, who, having the liberty to keep what he has, shall prove so unwise as to lose it."

Probably the best-known quote of the twentieth century American Christian missionary martyr Jim Elliot is "He is no fool who gives what he cannot keep, to gain that which he cannot lose." It seems likely that Jim Elliot had read *The Pilgrim's Progress* and was diametrically opposed in his opinion to that of fictional Mr. Hold-the-world in regard to which was the better investment, that made in this world or that made in the world to come.

Mr. Hold-the-world debates with fellow travelers Mr. Money-love, Mr. Save-all and Mr. By-ends about what they see as the excessive zeal and naivete of Christian and Hopeful. They see no reason for Christian forbearance or sacrifice, but believe that to amass wealth as a Christian, where possible, is a better investment that would serve a man well by making his disposition sweeter and motivating him to do more.

Even if you gained all the wealth and power of this world, and all the things it could offer you, yet lost your soul in the process, what good is that? —Luke 9:25 TPT

Jesus clearly taught that the gaining of wealth should not be accomplished to the detriment of the soul. Solomon taught that whoever loves money can never have enough (see Ecclesiastes 5:10). The apostle Paul concurred, saying that the love of money (and not money itself) is the root of all kinds of evil (see 1 Timothy 6:10) and explicitly cautioned that overseers should be free from the love of money (see 1 Timothy 3:3).

Rather, believers should lay up their treasures in heaven, where there will be no loss (see Matthew 6:20). This is the better investment that we all should be making.

- Why is amassing earthly wealth so attractive to so many?
- How can a strong desire for great worldly wealth lead to spiritual shipwreck?
- What investment are you making right now into your heavenly account?

Father, I pray that the love of money will be eradicated from my heart. May my desire to please You be stronger than any desire to gain earthly advantages or possessions. Grant me the grace and wisdom to bless others, thereby constantly storing up heavenly treasures to keep for eternity.

54 | A BETTER MOTIVE

Shechem had set his mind on Jacob's daughter and his cattle.

S ome follow Christ for personal gain, but there is no merit or true gain in seeking to follow Christ merely to marry or prosper. One should be ready to follow Christ no matter what may come. The benefits in following Christ are better than anything this world can offer, and the pursuit of them demands a better motive.

Christian mounts a strong and stinging rebuke to the reasoning of the four travelers from Fair-speech, who reason that God will smile on those who gain riches at the expense of some loss of righteousness. Christian exposes the mixed motives and actions of Shechem, a prince in Canaan who, while having strong attraction to Jacob's daughter, was also strongly fixated on the value of her father's cattle.

> Will their livestock and their property and all their animals not be ours? Let's just consent to them, and they will live with us. —Genesis 34:23 NASB

Shechem was not wrong to desire Jacob's daughter, but he was totally wrong to force sexual relations without her consent. Even in consensual relations where, say, a poor but beautiful young woman willingly marries a rich old man, the motive for their union is justifiably suspect. But Shechem's motives were base. There should be evidence of a better motive for each party before a marriage can be wholeheartedly celebrated.

Determining to follow Christ is more than any earthly marriage. Earthly marriage is dissolved by the death of one of the two parties. The marriage of believers who constitute the Bride of Christ, the one true Church, will be an everlasting covenant, and to enter it demands a better motive.

- What are your own motives for following Christ?
- How can earthly motives sometimes creep into Christian practice?
- What better motives should be the hallmark of true believers?

Father, search my heart and show me any motives that are unworthy in my pilgrimage toward an eternity with You. If ignoble motives are found in me, please purge them from my heart. Holy Spirit, influence my heart so that my motives are only the purest and highest, that my ways fully please You.

55 | A BETTER TREASURE

Here is a silver mine, and some digging in it for treasure.

Even in churches full of well-meaning believers, there are those rogues who spot a potential treasure trove in the trusting hearts of their fellow congregants. They are seeking earthly treasure in God's house when they ought to be seeking a better treasure.

After moving ahead of Mr. By-ends and his companions, Christian and Hopeful quickly pass through the delightful meadow called Ease. They then pass close to a hill called Lucre, where there is a silver mine kept by Demas, who lures travelers from the path to seek riches. The mine is unsafe, and many have died or become permanently maimed. Hopeful wants to seek riches at the mine, but Christian uses strong arguments and rebuke to counter the scheming arguments of Demas, and the pair pass by this considerable distraction.

> For Demas, having loved this present world, has deserted me and gone to Thessalonica. —2 Timothy 4:10 NASB

Demas was a man who had assisted the apostle Paul and Luke on a mission (see Colossians 4:14) but whose love for money later caused him to desert Paul (See 2 Timothy 4:10). Demas sought to build up his worldly treasure while neglecting a better treasure.

Our adversary Satan uses greed and covetousness to see if any can be pulled off track and then used to persuade others to join them where "the grass is greener." Some deceivers come from inside fellowships, or go to churches and use the trust networks there in an attempt to get rich quick. The only way to avoid deception is to rely on the Holy Spirit for discernment and keep one's focus fixed on Christ, who is our better treasure and sure hope of reward.

- Why do some have no care about who they deceive in order to enrich themselves?
- How by seeking treasure on earth can we end up losing treasure in heaven?
- How can your order of strategic priorities keep you from being deceived?

Father, may my conscience remain tender and fully alive so that I shall not be tempted to exploit others, or allow others to do so, in order to enrich my own self. Lead me toward storing up heavenly treasures as I make selfless sacrifices by the direction of Your Spirit.

They both concluded that this was the pillar of salt into which Lot's wife was turned, because of her looking back with a covetous heart.

Those who follow Christ ought to look forward and never turn back, as to do so would make them less worthy of a better promise.

Having narrowly escaped the distraction and danger of the silver mine, Christian and Hopeful spot what appears to be a monument of a woman changed into a pillar of salt. Looking more closely, Hopeful notices some writing in an ancient script that Christian is able to translate as saying, "Remember Lot's wife." Lot's wife had escaped destruction, but then looked back and was punished; in so doing, she missed out on a better promise of rescue and a new life.

> But Lot's wife, from behind him, looked back, and she became a pillar of salt. —Genesis 19:26 NASB

Lot's wife shows how much a little backsliding of heart can destroy a person in the end. Christ taught His disciples that anyone who put his hand to the plow and began working toward a harvest for eternal life ought never to turn back lest he be judged as unworthy (see Luke 9:62).

When Elijah called Elisha by casting his mantle upon him, he was happy to follow, but first requested a time to bid his parents farewell, and Elijah allowed his request (1 Kings 19:20). But in order for that mantle to rest permanently on his shoulders, Elisha had to set his face like flint and refuse to let Elijah out of his sight for another moment. Elisha's single-minded pursuit of what was needed made him the inheritor of a better promise (see 2 Kings 2:10–12).

- Why do you suppose the Lord is so sensitive to any backsliding?
- How can just a little backsliding lead to a great loss of reward?
- How can you be more confident of obtaining the rewards of a better promise?

Father, search my heart and reveal all waywardness in me. I humbly petition You to purge me from such unworthy tendencies and teach me how to become single-minded in my pursuit of Your presence and kingdom. Thank You for the work of the Holy Spirit, who makes me a partaker in that better promise of an eternity with You.

Indeed, what pleasant fruit and leaves these trees yield!

The Christian path is varied. There may be moments and periods of great trial or suffering, others of rather everyday experience, yet others that are unusually sweet and restorative. We would all tend toward wanting more of the latter. By God's grace the normal experience of a maturing Christian leads toward brighter days and better fruit (see Proverbs 4:18; John 15:5).

Christian and Hopeful journey on, and the path leads them beside a pleasant river that King David called the river of God (see Psalm 65:9). On either side of the river is an evergreen meadow and fruit trees bearing pleasant fruit and leaves that bring healing. They have several nights of full and safe rest in the meadow, with days spent eating fruits and gathering leaves.

> On either side of the river was the tree of life, bearing twelve kinds of fruit, yielding its fruit every month; and the leaves of the tree were for the healing of the nations. —Revelation 22:2 NASB

All the major cities of times past tended to be situated near water, and even if coastal, they were built around an estuary. Water from the river literally gave life to the city for drinking, washing and agriculture. In the book of Revelation, the apostle John saw the Celestial City, the new Jerusalem, and the river of the water of life that supplied that city flowed from out of the very throne of God! No wonder the trees of that city produced a better fruit. Christ described such a source, an internal well of life, that is available to every thirsty believer (see John 7:37–39), and the believer who is constantly drinking that water yields a better fruit (see Galatians 5:22–23).

- Why do you think Christian maturity tends to lead toward brighter days?
- What fruit does the living water of the Spirit produce in your life?
- How can you enter a virtuous cycle of constantly drinking the water of life?

Father, may my path lead me from the morning sun of accepting Christ toward an even brighter day of obedience and walking in the light of Your Word. May I learn to drink daily of that inner well of the Spirit and so be refreshed and made ever more fruitful.

Vain-confidence . . . not seeing the way before him,
fell into a deep pit.

When someone has low confidence, he or she will generally not be willing to take the small and acceptable risks that lead to greater reward. A person of generally good confidence may learn to swim, drive, camp, trade, run a business and manage relationships well. Consequently, that person will tend to fare reasonably well in life. Yet over-confidence, while it may enjoy spectacular short-term success, generally ends badly. A confidence that is grounded in the wisdom of God and the patience of Job (see Job 14:14) is a better confidence.

Christian and Hopeful leave the path that has become hard to pass through for the softer grass of By-path Meadow, as it appears to follow beside the course of the true path. Along the way they meet Vain-confidence, who assures them that their new path also leads straight to Celestial City. Vain-confidence charges ahead out of sight, and as day turns to darkness, he loses his way and falls in a pit. His confidence has proven vain, and the pilgrims need to recover a better confidence (see Hebrews 10:35).

Those who mislead the upright into an evil way will themselves fall into their own pit, but the blameless will attain prosperity.
—Proverbs 28:10 NABRE

This verse from Proverbs contains a warning for the over-confident or deceitful. If someone exhibits a confidence that misleads the righteous into going astray, then the Scripture warns that their own ways will end in downfall and trouble. On the contrary, those who lead, advise, guide or counsel others well with wisdom shall attain to prosperity. Those who are truly wise have a better confidence.

- How can we determine the appropriate level of confidence when making a choice?
- Why are we prone to look for an easier way when we already know the right path?
- How can we attain to the level of better confidence that belongs to the wise?

Father, by the inner direction of Your Spirit may I discern between right and wrong choices. Grant me strength to choose to remain in the right course even when the going gets tough. As I mature in You, may Your wise principles become ingrained in my decisions, leading to prosperity.

59 | A BETTER EXPECTATION

*Then said the Giant, "Tonight you have trespassed my
property, by trampling in and lying on my grounds,
and therefore you must come with me."*

Bereavement, a broken relationship, persecution, loss of a
business, being laid off or fired, legal proceedings, diagnosis of a terminal condition, or some other major disappointment or setback—any of these can give despair a lead position.
But a Christian must learn to triumph in all circumstances,
never give in to despair, but hold firmly to a better expectation.

Christian and Hopeful have now turned back toward the
right way. Exhausted after arduous efforts, they find a little
shelter in which to sleep, only to be rudely awakened by Giant
Despair, who arrests them and forces them to accompany
him. Rather than taking up their swords, whereby two could
chase ten thousand, they allow Giant Despair to drive them
further into darkness and suffering.

> You have removed lover and friend far from me. My acquaintances are in a hiding place. —Psalm 88:18 NASB

Several Christian writers have described what one might
call the "dark night of the soul." This may be a period when

one feels as if the heavens are closed up like brass or iron due to disobedience; or it may be for reasons that can only be guessed at; or for the purposes of God's glory (see Psalm 22:1–2, 22).

Moreover, Christians have no immunity to depression. At any point in time, a substantial percentage of any community is being challenged by issues affecting mental health. In such instances, we need to persevere, believing that the darkest point is just before the breaking of a new day (see Psalm 30:5), and to declare that God's will for us is to be sound in mind (2 Timothy 1:7) and so secure a better expectation.

- What can you identify that has potential to bring, or has brought you, despair?
- What might cause you, or perhaps has caused you, "a dark night of the soul"?
- How can hope and trusting in God's Word bring comfort and eventual light?

Father, in good times help me to prepare for the setbacks that are a normal part of life, but also, to reach out to others whose expectation has fallen. Show me if there are areas where I need to repent or trust You more in order to lift my expectation. Bring me out of darkness and despair into the comfort of Your glorious light.

60 | A BETTER SONG

Giant's wife, talking with her husband about them further, and understanding they were yet alive, did advise him to counsel them to commit suicide.

E ven when life looks futile, we must cry out to God for a way out, believing that He will surely hear us. We need to totally resist and overcome the temptation to give up and end things ourselves. We should have confidence that God will make a better and glorious way for all those who cry out to Him.

Diffidence is the wife of the Giant Despair. Learning the pilgrims have been imprisoned and starved, she advises her husband to beat them mercilessly and suggest that they commit suicide. Christian and Hopeful are in desperate straits when they find the resolve to pray, and in a very short time, they begin to realize a way out (see 1 Corinthians 10:13).

> I'd rather be suffocated, even dead, than live in these aching bones of mine. —Job 7:15 VOICE

The Bible doesn't dodge even the hardest issues of life. Deep, dark despair can unbalance the mind and lead to decisions that ought not to be made. At such seemingly hopeless times one needs a trusted counselor who is able to listen and offer hope and direction.

The apostle Paul and his companion Silas were in a real jam when they were imprisoned in a Roman jail. Somehow, they found inner strength and began to pray and sing songs of praise to the Lord, who quickly sent an earthquake that released not only them, but every prisoner in the jail. When the jailer saw what had happened, he was about to kill himself, but Paul assured him that they were all still present and he would not be punished. Paul and Silas, and then the jailer, each refused the song of sorrow and found a better song.

- What can you do when life looks hopeless?
- Who can help you overcome the negative thoughts that come with gloom?
- What song has lifted your spirit when it has been downcast?

Father, help me to have an action plan for combating hopelessness whenever it shows up. Help me to know who I can trust and turn to when life is hard. Train me so that I will pray and praise even during the toughest of times. You are my song and the joy of my salvation.

On Saturday, about midnight, they began to pray,
and continued in prayer till almost break of day.

When we find ourselves locked in by harsh circumstances, poor health, challenges, enemies or some combination that imprisons us in a "Doubting Castle," we must use the unfathomable resource of prayer.

Hopeful and Christian remember the secret of prayer, unseen by men. Deep down in a dark dungeon they couple it with praise, and in a short while God provides a miraculous loosening and freedom to them.

When Peter was locked up in prison, the early Church believers were earnestly engaged in the secret of prayer at Mary's house. God sent an angel to Peter, who was asleep and chained up between two soldiers, and loosed him (see Acts 12:5–7).

Similarly, Paul and Silas did not allow their own unjust imprisonment to dampen their devotion to God. They had been charged without evidence, allowed no opportunity to defend themselves and then treated as if they had been found guilty.

Now about midnight Paul and Silas were praying and singing hymns of praise to God. —Acts 16:25 NASB

The magistrate had ordered them to be beaten harshly and then delivered them to a very secure prison. Rather than weep at their unjustified abuse, they appear to have worshiped the Lord for being allowed to share in His sufferings. What was their secret? Surely it was their prayer that strengthened them so supernaturally.

What is our knee-jerk reaction to personal injustice? Do we look for the best no-win, no-fee lawyer? Do we pray for the Lord to strike our oppressor? The secret of prayer ought to make us more Christlike, as it did for Paul and Silas, who sought and saw the salvation of their oppressor and fellow prisoners.

- When has the secret of prayer brought you strength and eventual freedom?
- How can you avoid being overcome by harsh personal circumstances?
- In what present challenge or injustice can prayer make you more Christlike?

Father, when I am being tried and tested close to my limited abilities, help me to draw on the secret of prayer in order not to be overcome. Through prayer and surrender, allow me to become able to withstand adversity and stand during the trials and tribulations of my pilgrimage.

A key in Christian's bosom, called Promise, opens any lock in Doubting Castle.

Some have said that the Bible contains hundreds of promises, enough for every day of the year. While we may debate the number of promises, we ought not to debate their surety. Some are conditional promises that are only binding upon the Lord if we act in certain ways, but others are unconditional, meaning that we can always claim them. We must learn to live in such a way that every promise becomes available to us by faith in the Lord.

The two pilgrims have endured great sufferings locked in a dark dungeon within Doubting Castle before Christian suddenly calls to mind that he was given a master key to open any door. That key holds the secret of promise.

> Not one of the good promises which the LORD had made to the house of Israel failed; everything came to pass. —Joshua 21:45 NASB

When we face a difficulty or see another believer facing a challenge, we need to look for an appropriate promise and take hold of it by faith. For instance, suppose you feel all alone and helpless, then meditate upon the promise of Christ to never leave you without comfort but to send the Holy Spirit to be with you (see John 14:18). Remember that the secret of promise is to believe it.

Also remember that some promises are conditional. Christ promised to send the Spirit to those who ask His Father (see Luke 11:13); the apostle Peter and his companions declared that the Spirit is given by God to those who obey Him. To profit from a promise of God, we must believe it if it is unconditional (see Mark 16:17) and meet the conditions when it is conditional.

- What are a few key promises of God that He wants you to hold on to?
- Which promise do you need to believe to move forward in your journey?
- Does that promise have any conditions? If so, what are they?

Father, may I not become stuck and fail to progress when there is a promise in Your Word that can carry me much further forward. Teach me to mediate upon what You have done for others by that promise and to be willing to meet any conditions You have set.

The Shepherds, I say, whose names were
Knowledge, Experience, Watchful, and Sincere,
took them by the hand.

How do you determine if something is good for you or not? Did you know that some wild mushrooms are edible while others are poisonous? If you didn't know which kind you had before eating it, you could become ill. That is the secret of the mystery of the mushroom, and knowing it well separates what is poisonous from what is good food.

The pilgrims' journey takes them high upon the Delectable Mountains, where they meet four Shepherds whom they question about the way ahead and the owner of the mountains. Then the Shepherds question them, and finding them sincere pilgrims, they show them the wonders of the mountains. The Shepherds unveil the secret of the mystery of each wonder, showing that the path is safe walking for the sincere pilgrim but dangerous for the sinner who would stumble.

> But solid food is for the mature, who because of practice have their senses trained to distinguish between good and evil.
> —Hebrews 5:14 NASB

Like knowing how to select an edible mushroom, the mature believer has learned what things in life are nourishment to the soul and what things are poisonous to it. The writer to the Hebrews was chastising the readers that they were still consuming only baby milk at an age in their spiritual lives when they ought to be preparing and enjoying healthy solid foods.

It is normal for children to want to eat the same foods as the adults around them once they have grown teeth. The secret of the mystery of baby teeth is that they push through the gums and last until the jaw grows too big, and then adult teeth push through behind them. While it is mysterious, such growth is normal.

- Why is the path safe for sincere pilgrims but dangerous for sinners?
- How can a believer learn to prepare and enjoy solid food from the Bible?
- How does the Holy Spirit help you to distinguish between good and evil?

Father, thank You that You have filled this earth with mysteries that the wise are able to unravel. Thank You that if I walk in the light of Your Word, I shall not stumble. Teach me to prepare and feed myself with Your solid Word, and train me to discern rightly and live righteously.

They first led them to the top of a hill called Error,
which was very steep on the furthest side.

Christian doctrine has been plagued by heresies since the very earliest days of the Church. What is crucial to know is that the essence of truth is in a Person and not in a set of beliefs. That Person, who is Truth, is Christ, and His Spirit, who will guide us into all truth, is available to the submitted believer (see John 16:13). Knowing Christ personally and following Him as Lord and Savior is the secret of the truth.

The four Shepherds lead Christian and Hopeful to the top of a hill called Error. When they look down the steep side, they see several men dashed to pieces below. The Shepherds explain that these were men whose doctrines led them to their own destruction.

Men . . . have gone astray from the truth, claiming that the resurrection has already taken place; and they are jeopardizing the faith of some. —2 Timothy 2:18 NASB

Nobody begins to follow Christ intending to go astray, but if we forget that we have an active enemy, Satan, the opposer of our souls, then we may end up mistaking his voice for that voice of the Spirit (see 2 Corinthians 2:11; 11:14).

There is a delicate balance that needs to be learned between discerning the voice of the Holy Spirit and studying the Bible to discern scriptural truths. Some, thinking they have clearly heard the Spirit, have not rigorously studied the Scriptures for confirmation, while others who have rigorously studied the Scriptures have not submitted to the correction of the Spirit. To maintain the proper balance between scriptural study—including that obtained by sitting under biblical teaching—and the confirming voice of the Spirit is to maintain the secret the of truth.

- What are some of the principal causes of heresies in the Church?
- What are some possible dangers that following heresies can lead to?
- How do you discern the teaching of the Spirit and confirm it by the Scriptures?

Father, there have been heresies from the beginning and there are many more in my day. May careful study of Your Word, and careful heeding of Your Spirit who shall direct me in the right path, lead me into greater personal knowledge of Your Son Christ, who is the Truth.

*After keeping them for some time in his dungeon, he gouged
out their eyes before leading them among those tombs,
where he left them wandering until now.*

A walking instructor tells those setting off, "Now,
please hear me carefully or you're going to feel it."
She then tells them about how they must wear thick socks
and boots that fit, keep their feet as dry as possible and stay
away from the edge of the path. When you heed the counsel
of a godly parent or mentor to obey the laws of God, walk
in His ways and prosper, then you are engaging the secret of
heeding (see 1 Chronicles 22:12–13).

The Shepherds lead them to Mount Caution, where they
see blinded men stumbling among tombstones. The two pilgrims had personally experienced the enticing detour that
led to Doubting Castle. When the Shepherds explain what
happened to others who had taken that way, they weep. It had
been a close escape, but Christian and Hopeful were taught
more of the secret of heeding.

A person who wanders from the way of understanding will rest
in the assembly of the dead. —Proverbs 21:16 NASB

This Scripture gives a morbid and solemn warning that careless living often ends in premature death, and if left unchecked, it eventually leads to eternal separation from God and His chosen ones (see Psalm 1:5–6).

It is better for you to learn the secret of heeding and enjoy God's approval and blessings early in life than to spend painful times undergoing His chastisement (see Hebrews 12:6). Our God is very gracious, and He does not punish us as we deserve. Once we seek His forgiveness and restoration, He is quick to show us abundant mercy (see Isaiah 55:7).

- What times in life have you had to feel it before you understood it?
- In what areas do you know that you need to surrender to God today?
- Who is someone you can share the secret of heeding with today?

Father, correction is never a pleasant experience, but I want to thank You for bringing correction to my attitudes, thoughts and behaviors when it was needed. Search my heart and show me any area that needs to be fully surrendered. Holy Spirit, empower me to heed Your voice, and help me to teach others the blessings of Your ways.

66 | THE SECRET OF LOYALTY

This is a byway to hell, a way that hypocrites go in at.

Hypocrisy is a breach of loyalty to the truth. A hypocrite is someone who professes a certain belief but whose actions demonstrate that this profession is not maintained with conviction. Christ saved His harshest condemnation of all for hypocrites. Christ Himself is the Way and the Truth, so to avoid His harshest criticism, you must learn the secret of loyalty.

The Shepherds show Christian and Hopeful the side of a hill from where they hear cries of torment and smell burning brimstone. The Shepherds warn them that these terrible cries come from those who acted disloyally and sold their birthright before reaching Celestial City.

> The priest shall order them to pull out the stones with the spot on them and throw them away at an unclean place outside the city. —Leviticus 14:40 NASB

A house suspected of leprosy in the days of ancient Israel would be inspected by the priest, and if a spot was found in a

140

wall that had spread after seven days, the priest would order every leprous stone to be torn out of the wall and thrown outside the city. According to the apostle Peter, each believer is a stone in a living house (see 1 Peter 2:5). Christ is sanctifying each believer in the Church so that this spiritual house may be without any spot [of sin] or wrinkle, according to the apostle Paul (see Ephesians 5:26–27).

Loyalty to Christ means remaining attached to Him, being cleansed by His words and obeying His commands (see John 15:3, 10). If we do not remain attached, we will wither, be gathered and then cast into the fire (see John 15:6). How much better to learn the secret of loyalty.

- What is the difference between making mistakes and hypocrisy?
- What are the benefits of loyalty to Christ?
- What does John 15 say is the secret to abiding or remaining in Christ?

Father, may Your Spirit convict me of areas where my conduct is not what You desire from me. Teach me how to live a holy life so that sin does not hinder Your calling on my life. Abide in me as I abide in You, that I may bear much fruit, showing myself to be a disciple of Christ and glorifying the Father.

Guilt, with a great club that was in his hand, struck Little-faith
on the head, and with that blow felled him flat on the
ground, where he lay bleeding.

Guilt acts as a depressant in the life of anyone. Guilt can knock you to the ground bruised and bleeding and leave you in a place of despair. The only sure way to overcome guilt is by first obtaining and then keeping a clear conscience.

Along the path Christian remembers a story about Little-faith, from a town called Sincere, who once slept nearby along the same pilgrim pathway. He awoke to find himself being repeatedly beaten by Guilt. Little-faith might never have survived that ordeal had it not been for the sound of approaching footsteps that caused Guilt to run away.

> Jesus answered, "Those who have had a bath need only to wash their feet; their whole body is clean." —John 13:10 NIV

Christ taught His disciples that they were clean except for their feet, which required washing. Christ was saying that they were saved, but in their daily walk their feet sometimes strayed from the good path and became dirty. Christ was teaching us that each day we need to repent and be cleansed from sins committed during that day. By cleansing our sin daily, guilt has no time to accumulate, and we have learned the secret of a clear conscience.

As believers, we need to train ourselves to discern between when the devil is accusing us but there is no case to answer (see Revelation 12:10), and when the Spirit is convicting us of sin and we need to earnestly repent (see John 16:8). By correctly discerning, and repenting when convicted by the Spirit, we shall know the secret of a clear conscience.

- What have you observed or experienced about the debilitating effects of guilt?
- How will daily repentance protect you from living under a dark cloud of guilt?
- What benefits will you reap by learning the secret of a clear conscience?

Father, may my life not be darkened by a cloud of personal guilt. Rather, let me daily repent and seek forgiveness and cleansing from You for wrong actions from the recent past. Today, help me walk in the love of God, the grace of the Lord Jesus Christ and the power of the Spirit.

Esau sold his birthright, his greatest jewel, for a mere bowl of red lentil stew. If Esau sold out for nothing, why wouldn't Little-faith do so too?

Christ told a parable of a man who discovered treasure in a field and then hid it again before going and selling all that he had to buy the field (see Matthew 13:44). The secret of a little faith in that great treasure made him risk all the little that he had to achieve far greater gain.

Little-faith, having been robbed by Mistrust and beaten by Guilt, had escaped by God's mercies, and somehow retained his certificate and his jewels. He was left without change to spend along the way, and his jewels were not considered of much value where he was. But Little-faith was content to go hungry and beg, rather than sell what he had left, because he knew the value of what he had retained. That was the secret of Little-faith.

No one should be immoral or godless like Esau, who sold his birthright for a single meal. —Hebrews 12:16 ISV

Here is a stark and clear warning. What simple and temporary earthly satisfaction is worth grabbing when the price is the loss of your eternal salvation? How would you dare to act in such a presumptuous, shortsighted and foolish way?

A little faith is all that is necessary to overcome. Christ taught that a word of command, mixed with only your little faith, will move a mountain (see Mark 11:23). The psalmist taught that those who trust in the Lord shall be as unmovable as Mount Zion (see Psalm 125:1). The psalmist did not specify the level of trust required, whether great or small; he only specified where the trust must be placed, in the Lord. That is the secret of a little faith.

- Where is your greatest treasure hidden? And what is it?
- What would you never trade or sell? Why?
- How can you ensure that your faith, however small, is placed in the Lord?

Father, help me to know what is truly valuable in life. May I learn that the saving faith that has been entrusted to me must never be sold, buried or bartered. Teach me by the express guidance of Your Holy Spirit how to place my little faith wholly in You.

It is Flatterer, a false apostle, who has transformed himself into an angel of light.

A stereotype of men is that when driving somewhere, they assume that they know the way. Consequently, men who are unwilling to ask directions more often end up taking the scenic route! How much time, fuel and embarrassment could have been saved if only they had paused and asked for direction? Knowing that you don't know is part of the secret of humility.

Having been sent on their way with a note from the Shepherds, which they did not stop to read, the pilgrims reach a fork in the road and are uncertain which path to choose. Along comes Flatterer, in disguise as a good man, and he tells them to follow him to Celestial City. They follow, but he leads them into a trap, and they only escape when a Shining One cuts them free. They have not yet learned the secret of humility.

A man who flatters his neighbor is spreading a net for his steps.
—Proverbs 29:5 NASB

"Beware when all men speak well of you," Christ warned the crowd (see Luke 6:26). Christ knew the danger of being carried by men's praise rather than by God's approval. The praise of others will puff you up, but to obtain God's approval you must voluntarily humble yourself, even if receiving a torrent of earthly praise. When you enjoy the praise of others, seeking to maintain it will lead you away from the truth.

When you trust in your own wisdom, you will become a falling fool, but when you walk in the true wisdom of God you will be safe (see Proverbs 28:26). An essential part of the wisdom that you need to acquire is the secret of humility.

- When has false confidence or misdirection by others caused you to miss the way?
- How would you advise someone you care for about how to escape a flatterer?
- How can you acquire and safeguard the secret of humility?

Father, save me from false confidence in myself or others. Help me to know where I can find sound and honest direction. Keep me from drinking from the sweet cup of the flatterer that will later turn bitter. Teach me Your ways so that I may walk faithfully in humility.

Christian replied, "We are going to Mount Zion."
Then Atheist fell into a very great laughter.

Confidence in a person or a truth is good if it is well placed. The difficulty is in discerning the hearts of men and the wisdom of their thoughts. As we grow in our knowledge of God, and our reverent appreciation of Him and His ways, we shall acquire the secret of confidence.

Shortly after being set back on the true path by the Shining One, the pilgrims see a man coming toward them with his back to Celestial City. As he meets them, he inquires where they are headed. At their reply, he laughs and tells them he is returning from a fruitless quest of twenty years to find Celestial City, and he has determined that there is no such place. The pilgrims deliberate, but then determine to walk by faith and not by sight.

> Now he went up from there to Bethel; and as he was going up by the road, some young boys came out from the city and ridiculed him and said to him, "Go up, you baldhead; go up, you baldhead!" —2 Kings 2:23 NASB

One of the first encounters that the newly anointed prophet Elisha had was with some young people who openly mocked him for having a bald head. No matter how anointed you are, you must expect opposition and even ridicule. Christ Himself bore such opposition and scorn at the cross when some jeered, "He saved others; let Him save Himself" (Luke 23:35 NASB). But Christ's last recorded words by Luke were "Father, into your hands I commit my spirit" (Luke 23:46 NIV). Being able to press forward steadily in the face of doubt, fear, ridicule or even a sense of abandonment is the secret of confidence.

- How can you know if your confidence in a person or truth has been well placed?
- How should you handle questions that are designed to shipwreck your confidence?
- What can you learn from Christ about how never to lose confidence in God?

Father, open the eyes of my understanding so that I can rightly see others and weigh truths. Grant me great understanding so that the hostile remarks and questions that are directed at me can be sent back with confident wisdom that will turn even the hearts of enemies toward You.

What! No Mount Zion? Didn't we see the gate of the city
from the Delectable Mountains? Also, are we not now
to walk by faith?

Christians profess certain faith in God, while atheists
profess certainty that there is no God and are no gods.
Agnostics are only sure that they cannot be sure whether a
deity or deities exist, or if that is even knowable.

Atheist tells the pilgrims that after twenty years of searching, he is sure that the whole concept of a place called Celestial
City is nothing but fiction. The pilgrims have nothing left to
contest that except their own faith. They recall that from the
Delectable Mountains they both glimpsed the doors of the
Celestial City through the telescope. They then determine that
the strength of their own belief is enough to press forward.

For we walk by faith, not by sight. —2 Corinthians 5:7 NASB

Three men were walking in the desert for a long time until
they had no more water. Upon seeing a great palace come
into view, the first declared, "It is a mirage; it's not real." The
second declared, "I cannot be sure it is real. I'm exhausted;

let me stay here and die." The third declared, "I know it; it's the palace my father built. We are saved!" The first is like the atheist, the second like the agnostic, and you, dear believer, are like the third one.

For many Christians the early days of believing were marked by a gracious revelation of God. There may have been a seemingly impossible situation where a miracle took place. But as our faith grows, our priorities and focus become less on this life and more on what is beyond its boundaries. We learn to walk by faith.

- How do you deal with doubts concerning your faith in God?
- How can your faith alone become sufficient motive for you to press forward?
- What do you do when confronted by those who do not see by faith?

Father, may I never be timid to share my doubts with You; I know You can handle them. Teach me how to walk by faith. Help me to look more toward life in eternity, increasingly embracing heavenly values and becoming less concerned with the challenges and issues of this life.

72 | THE SECRET OF WATCHFULNESS

Christian reminded Hopeful, "Do you not remember that one of the Shepherds warned us about the Enchanted Ground? He specifically meant that we should beware of sleeping."

The Bible tells us that the ruler of the kingdom of this world is at work in the spirits of the disobedient and that we used to obey him (see Ephesians 2:2). Old habits have a habit of coming back, so we need to be vigilant to avoid returning to old ungodly lifestyles. We must avoid falling asleep spiritually by learning the secret of watchfulness.

The two pilgrims reach a certain country where the air makes them become naturally drowsy. Hopeful longs for sleep, and Christian has to rebuke him sharply and remind him of the Shepherd's warning not to sleep on Enchanted Ground.

> So then, let's not sleep as others do, but let's be alert and sober.
> —1 Thessalonians 5:6 NASB

Paul was reminding the believers at Thessalonica that they should be living in the expectation of Christ's return. Paul taught them that the world was living carelessly, not believing the gospel or that Christ will return. Paul taught that we as believers ought to be living with spiritual alertness so that, when Christ returns, we will not be surprised or caught off guard.

Living with spiritual alertness means "living in the light." Jesus taught that He had to work the works of God His Father while there was still daylight because no one can work at night (see John 9:4). (There was no electricity then!) Christ meant that while we have grace and strength to do good and please our heavenly Father, we should do so with zeal. Making the best use of our time is part of the secret of watchfulness.

- Why do we need to actively resist the tendency to go back to old habits?
- How can the world live in such a carefree way, while we cannot afford to?
- In what ways can you be watchful today and work while it is day?

Father, may a godly zeal arise in my heart today that will propel me forward in my walk with You. May I reflect upon why I need to be watchful knowing that one day Christ will return for His Church and that my opportunities for doing good are not unlimited.

73 | THE SECRET OF SOUL CARE

Hopeful sought to clarify Christian's question, "Do you mean, how did I first come to look after the good of my soul?"

A seasoned traveler has learned to carry only the bare necessities and to leave behind nonessentials that would otherwise add unnecessary weight. To become a seasoned Christian pilgrim you must learn, by practical experience of their relative importance, what those essentials are.

Far into their pilgrimage, and traveling through Enchanted Ground, the priority of the two pilgrims is to stay alert. They determine to resist sleep by engaging in profitable conversation and fellowship. The first topic they choose is that of how Hopeful began to see the need to care for his soul.

> Beloved, I pray that in all respects you may prosper and be in good health, just as your soul prospers. —3 John 1:2 NASB

The apostle John made a direct link between the well-being of a believer and the state of his or her soul. We need to see that connection clearly as a spiritual principle before we can grasp the imperative and begin to learn the secret of soul care.

Once you have taken hold of the secret of soul care, you will see that the Bible is your map and your daily food, the Holy Spirit is your companion and your living water, readiness in the gospel is your walking shoes, prayer is your torch, Christ is your Shepherd, and the Father is your Guarantor whenever you need supplies. Your duty is to care for your soul, nourishing it in the Word, resting as the Shepherd directs and strengthening yourself in fellowship with your God and fellow believers. All these will be essentials for you if you have learned the secret of soul care.

- Why should daily care of your soul be such a top priority?
- Why do some fail to see the need of taking care of their souls?
- What are some of the essentials that you must carry with you?

Father, may the imperative and the secret of soul care be revealed to me, becoming deeply ingrained in my innermost and dearest values and practices. May I become seasoned in using all the essential kit of knowing and trusting Your Word, prayer, fellowship, witnessing and yielding to the Holy Spirit.

> *Hopeful responded, "I thought I must endeavor to reform my life; for otherwise, I thought, I am certain to end up eternally lost."*

The concept of grace is hard to accept. It may at first appear to be something for nothing, but it is most certainly not that. Grace means we receive great favor at no cost to ourselves, but at a very great cost to Christ, who has paid the full price of our sin.

Hopeful explains how for a while his attempts to reform his life—together with religiously praying, reading and repenting—gave him reason to hope. But all this did not stop his conviction of being a helpless sinner. Then his friend Faithful had explained that Christ freely received a punishment that He never deserved so that Hopeful could receive a forgiveness that he never deserved and be fully justified. That's the secret of grace.

> Nevertheless, knowing that a person is not justified by works of the Law but through faith in Christ Jesus, even we have believed in Christ Jesus, so that we may be justified by faith in Christ and not by works of the Law; since by works of the Law no flesh will be justified. —Galatians 2:16 NASB

Grace involves your obtaining a personal knowledge of these truths. First, you must know that no amount of future good works can ever remove the penalty of your past sin. Second, you must know that because of His great love for you, Christ died in your place at Calvary to pay the price for all your sin, past, present and future. Third, you must be sure that if you accept what Christ did for you and determine to trust and serve Him, you will be saved. Finally, you must act upon what the Holy Spirit has revealed to you.

- How would you describe grace to somebody who asks?
- What sorts of things might you be tempted to do to supplement grace?
- Why is it that grace alone is sufficient for your salvation?

Father, help me to meditate upon the workings of grace in my life. May I realize that I can never, nor could ever, save myself or live righteously on my own, and so I shall always be indebted to Your grace in my life. May I do good works that come out of a grateful heart, fully in Your amazing grace.

| THE SECRET OF
IDENTIFICATION

Faithful told me, "You must be justified by him, even by trusting in what he alone did, all by himself, in the days of his humanity, when he suffered by hanging on the cross."

A compact explanation of justification is given as "just as if I'd never sinned." It won't satisfy every theologian, but it does help get to the core of what the process of justification brings about for you as a believer.

Faithful needed to teach Hopeful the secret of identification. His old identification was of a hopeless sinner who would certainly be condemned to hell. Hopeful could see that Christ was a perfect man who deserved heaven. The gap between his sinful life and Christ's perfect life seemed unbridgeable, until he understood that Christ took his sin and became as a sinner so that he could receive Christ's righteousness and become as a perfect man.

> But now having been freed from sin and enslaved to God, you derive your benefit, resulting in sanctification, and the outcome, eternal life. —Romans 6:22 NASB

What a wonderfully liberating truth Paul is sharing in Romans 6. He is teaching that by faith in Christ you can be justified before God, because the penalty for your sin has been paid, and your pardon purchased by the perfect sacrifice of Christ on your behalf.

Sin used to be like a deadweight around your life, dragging you down and holding you in slavery. But Christ has taken the weight, and you have been cut free. Not only have you been cut free, but your dead soul has been resurrected (see Ephesians 2:1, 5), and you have been washed in His precious blood (see Revelation 1:5) and sealed with His Holy Spirit so that you are now counted as holy and acceptable before God (see Ephesians 1:13).

- How would you explain the secret of identification?
- How does it make you feel to know that your sins have been forgiven?
- What positive changes have occurred because of your salvation?

Father, thank You that my old identity has been erased at the cross and a new identity was transferred to me as Your child. Thank You that my sins have been forgiven, the deadweight of guilt has been removed and I am born again, free and walking by the Spirit today.

But, Lord, can such a great sinner as I am really be accepted and be saved by you?

Many may fear they are beyond saving. "I'm too old now." "If you only knew what I have done." "I'll just have to take my chances now." Endless excuses. But Jesus holds no excuse for rejecting you, because He has promised to accept every sinner who turns to Him in sincerity, humility and brokenness. If you haven't pleaded your case yet, then what are you waiting for?

Hopeful tells Christian how he begged for God to forgive him of his sins and save him many times, and how he would have given up, except that he could see no other way out from certain condemnation. Then one day he saw Christ through the eyes of faith and reasoned with Him as to whether he could ever be saved. Christ gave Hopeful many assurances of His willingness and confirmed that the very reason He came into the world was to bring salvation to sinners.

All whom My Father has given to Me will come to Me. I will never turn away anyone who comes to Me. —John 6:37 NLV

What a marvelous encouragement we have from Christ Himself to come to Him as Savior and Lord. He has a policy of accepting all candidates. Every applicant can become gainfully employed in the great work of building His Kingdom.

Have you made excuses for why you cannot respond to God's call upon your life? You can't say He hasn't asked or doesn't want you or can't help you. Christ and His great love mean the end of excuses.

- Why might you be tempted to believe you are not worthy of salvation?
- Why might the Lord sometimes allow us to cry out more than once?
- What are the benefits of accepting Christ's invitation to come and be saved?

Father, my life is Yours. I thank You that Christ left the comforts of heaven to be born as a baby and grow as a man enduring much opposition, temptation, suffering and death on the cross in order that I could be forgiven, cleansed, saved, healed and Spirit-filled.

*It made me love a holy life, and long to do something
for the honor and glory of the name of the Lord Jesus.*

The realization of how abhorrent your unredeemed life
was before your salvation is a powerful motive not to
ever return to it. In fact, if your feet should slip along the pathway, and you are convicted and repent, then it should create
in you an urgency to show your displeasure with the wrong
you have done by doing much right (see 2 Corinthians 7:11).

The experience of seeing Christ and hearing Him through
his spiritual senses caused Hopeful to recognize four fundamentals: (1) the world is condemned through sin; (2) God
justly justifies those who trust in Christ; (3) the condition of
an unrepentant sinner is shameful and vile; and (4) he, having been saved, wanted to remain holy and live for God. His
life could never be the same again; he had reached the end
of the ordinary.

> If you keep yourself pure, you will be a special utensil for honorable use. Your life will be clean, and you will be ready for the
> Master to use you for every good work. —2 Timothy 2:21 NLT

Paul instructed his son in the Lord, Timothy, how to become a person the Lord would use for special assignments. Paul had certainly learned how to qualify, and if you follow his advice to Timothy, it will lead to the end of the ordinary!

What must you do? You must keep yourself pure. Not hours of study, days of fasting, nights of prayer, but keeping yourself pure and living a holy life are all that are required. This requires submitting to the leading of the Holy Spirit wherever and in whatever He directs you.

- What attitudes and behaviors should recognition of your past condition lead to?
- What led Hopeful to a state where he wanted to remain holy and live for God?
- How can you become God's chosen vessel and reach the end of the ordinary?

Father, may I never forget the dark and desperate condition You saved me from. May the memory of where You took me from create in me the desire to stay holy and live for You. May Your Spirit lead me to live a pure and extraordinary life for the honor and glory of the name of Jesus.

78 | THE END OF IGNORANCE

Ignorance protested, "I will never believe that my heart is so bad."

An ignorant person is one who ignores what should be known or obvious. Suppose you speed in your vehicle and a police officer stops you and informs you of your offence. You say truthfully, "I am sorry, officer, I had no idea what the speed limit was." The officer is likely to reply, "I am sorry, but by law, ignorance is no valid excuse."

When the pilgrims meet Ignorance again, Christian asks him how he can trust his own heart, and Ignorance replies that he can trust his heart because it is good. Christian points out what the Scripture teaches—that the heart of man is continually inclined toward evil (see Genesis 6:5), even from youth (see Genesis 8:21), so his own judgment of himself cannot be trustworthy. He has not reached the end of Ignorance.

> Therefore no one will be declared righteous in God's sight by the works of the law; rather, through the law we become conscious of our sin. —Romans 3:20 NIV

The Bible teaches that no man, woman or child, including you, can be justified before God on account of their good behavior. Yet so many, when asked why they expect or hope to get to heaven, say something like, "Well, my neighbors are churchgoing, Bible-believing Christians, and my house is a lot more peaceful than theirs. If they're so sure of going, I'm looking good." Such a statement shows that the end of ignorance has not yet been reached.

Ignorance only ends when the heart surrenders to facts and faces hard truths. When you confess your absolute need of Christ and His work on the cross, and you surrender to His will, then you have reached the end of ignorance.

- When has ignorance been offered as an excuse recently in your life?
- What has caused the heart that is not surrendered to become so untrustworthy?
- What are you doing to ensure ignorance is kept far from your heart?

Father, it is so easy to lean on ignorance and offer it up as a reason for mercy to be shown. Help me to surrender my heart and mind unconditionally and wholly to You, that You may teach me Your ways, Your principles, and lead me in paths of righteousness.

Ignorance exclaimed, "What! Would you have us trust in only what Christ has done, without us?"

As humans, we have a natural tendency to want to justify our actions, even when we know they are not justifiable. The first step to you becoming a Christian is for you to admit you are a sinner. The second step is to believe that you can only be saved by the atoning work of Christ. The third step is to confess Christ as your personal Lord and Savior, knowing your own righteousness is worthless. Then you may be led by the Holy Spirit on the path to the end of childishness.

Christian and Ignorance continue their lively discussion. Ignorance believes that his own inadequate good works were made good by Christ's death, making him a candidate for heaven. Christian explains that this is (1) unscriptural, (2) based on the righteousness of Ignorance, (3) an attempt to justify his deeds but not his person, and (4) deceitful and ineffective. When asked to believe only in the saving work of Christ, Ignorance is offended!

What shall we say then? Shall we continue in sin that grace may abound? —Romans 6:1 NKJV

Some take offense upon understanding the gospel of grace, a free pardon of all sin (without any good deeds of the believer needed for salvation). They are not ready to admit how much they need help and that there is nothing they can do to help themselves. It is the first stage of most successful addict recovery programs to publicly admit the problem you have. If you do not pass through that point of honesty that brings necessary humiliation, you will not arrive at the end of childishness.

But the end of childishness is so sweet as it leads us into a proper growing and ongoing walk and relationship with Jesus.

- Why might you prefer to make excuses rather than to own up?
- What is so wrong with trusting in your own goodness for salvation?
- What habits have you formed to avoid childish behavior in your daily walk?

Father, may today be an end of excuses in my life. Search my life and show me any areas where it is time for me to own up and take responsibility. Help me to trust only in You and Your promises. I want to mature in Christ and walk in both the fruit and power of the Spirit.

80 | THE END OF UNCERTAINTY

No man can know Jesus Christ except by the revelation of the Father.

Before grace imparted faith, it would have been impossible for you to truly know God or any of the mysteries of the Christian faith. That is why the knowledge of God, His salvation, His forgiveness, His person and His power are hidden from the minds of unbelievers (see John 12:40). It is by grace alone that you acquire saving knowledge of Christ and the Father and are saved; it is not by any effort or action on your part (see Ephesians 2:8).

Christian firmly asserts that Ignorance is a man whose name accurately describes who he is. He declares Ignorance to be ignorant (1) of how justification is completed by trusting in the righteousness of Christ, (2) that only such trust can save a soul from judgment, and (3) of how true saving faith makes the believer love Christ, His name, His Word, His ways and His people.

True faith and love for God release His mighty power, bringing transformation into the mind, soul and life of the believer, a transformation that causes the end of uncertainty.

All things have been handed over to Me by My Father; and no one knows the Son except the Father; nor does anyone know the Father except the Son, and anyone to whom the Son determines to reveal Him. —Matthew 11:27 NASB

Christ asserted that only He knew God the Father, who had handed Him the power to reveal the Father to others; therefore, He was the only way to the Father (see John 14:6). The certain knowledge of salvation is not found in any other major faith. Only Christianity can allow you to be sure that you are saved (see John 5:24; 1 John 5:13). True faith in Christ that leads to loving, trusting, obeying and serving Him brings the end of uncertainty.

- Why do you think God reveals Himself to some but not to others?
- How did Ignorance suppose he would be saved?
- How can you be sure that you are saved?

Father, thank You that You will not hide Yourself or Your salvation from those who earnestly seek You and recognize their need for Your salvation. Thank You that You will reveal Your salvation to those who, hungering and thirsting for righteousness, cry out to You. Grant me more revelation today.

... making it afraid to turn from them, to the right hand or to the left, to anything that may dishonor God, break its peace, grieve the Spirit, or cause the enemy to speak reproachfully.

Have you noticed in your own life or perhaps that of other believers a persistent inconsistency between the teachings of the faith and the life lived? How can someone with such a disconnect become more congruent and connected? How can the end of inconsistency be brought about?

Ignorance allows the pilgrims to proceed ahead, claiming he cannot keep pace with them. As soon as they part ways, Christian and Hopeful begin to discuss the pitiful condition of those like Ignorance. The pilgrims note that the challenge of pilgrimage arouses earthly fears in such people who have not learned righteous fear. Righteous fear begins with conviction of sin, which drives the soul to Christ for salvation, which then produces humility, tenderness and a daily dependence on the Lord. These characteristics form the foundation that will lead you to the end of inconsistency.

> The fear of the LORD is the beginning of wisdom, and the knowledge of the Holy One is understanding. —Proverbs 9:10 NASB

Godly fear is a key to progress. Godly fear does not mean being afraid of the person of God, but rather being afraid of the consequences of going against His directives and principles. The fear of not heeding is not so much due to a fear of punishment but more due to having the wisdom to know that going against God's ways leads to loss and ruin, while conforming to them leads to gain and honor.

This godly fear then leads to a correct relating to God, which in turn leads to an increase in the knowledge of the Holy One and His ways, which brings with it great understanding.

- What changes in attitude are required before a Christian can walk consistently?
- How would you explain godly fear to a new Christian?
- What must you learn to practice before you can grow in understanding?

Father, teach me to have a holy reverence for You and the honor of Your name. May Your Spirit lead me to walk in the wisdom of heaven with humility, tenderness and daily dependence upon You. May my walk with You become ever closer that I may grow in understanding.

82 | THE END OF THE TEMPORARY

Hopeless affirmed it, "Know him? Yes, Temporary dwelt in Graceless, a town about two miles off of Honesty, and he dwelt next door to one Turnback."

The apostle Paul, in defending the ministry he and Timothy carried out, recounted how great a price they had paid to obey their call, and declared that their focus was not on visible temporary matters but rather on invisible eternal matters (see 2 Corinthians 4:18). The warning "You should look where you're going!" is helpful. Are you laboring toward some temporary home? Or are you pressing toward an eternal dwelling?

As they draw near to the end of the Enchanted Ground, the conversation between Christian and Hopeful turns to a certain character called Temporary who lived in Graceless. Christian knew him and recalls that he had begun to come under conviction of sin and looked set to begin his pilgrimage when he became acquainted with Save-self, and then he suddenly fell away. That was the end of Temporary.

For by grace you have been saved through faith; and this is not of yourselves, it is the gift of God. —Ephesians 2:8 NASB

Salvation is freely obtained by faith in Christ. It can never be earned, because the price is beyond what man can afford. Yet it is freely given as a gift to those who repent of sin and ask God for forgiveness of their sins.

The moment you receive the gift of salvation is the same moment your dead spirit receives new life (see Ephesians 2:1, 5), and it is also the moment you pass from being condemned to death to having everlasting life (see John 5:24). If you are a true believer, then you have already begun to taste the end of the temporary.

- What characterizes a person who lives in Graceless?
- Why do some who seem to follow Christ later fall away (see Matthew 13:18–22)?
- How much are you focused on the age to come, and how do you know it?

Father, may my heart value Your salvation above all the treasures and vanities of earth. May my heart be as good ground that takes in Your Word and hides it until it produces a rich harvest. May my eyes be fixed upon Jesus the Forerunner, waiting at the finish line.

Just give this man his freedom, and he will be a thief, and still
such a rogue, whereas, if his mind was transformed,
he would be different.

Matter tends to return to its most natural state. In most of the earth, water is liquid, yet in the warm jungle much is a steamy mist, and in the subzero Antarctic much is ice. A sinner is no different—surrounded by the warmth of fervent saints, he may behave well; surrounded by villains, he becomes base; but in his most natural state he simply walks with the world in disobedience to God (see Ephesians 2:2).

Hopeful identifies four causes of starting out with God and making an about-turn: (1) an initial fear and fervor that subsides; (2) a fear of what men think and how much it might cost you to continue; (3) not wanting to endure the insults and ridicule that those who follow the Lord closely will suffer; (4) a wish to rid yourself of troublesome thoughts of personal guilt or the Lord's judgment. Christian summarizes all these as a failure from the outset to fully change your mind and fully embrace true faith.

This is so because the corrupt nature has a hostile attitude toward God. It refuses to place itself under the authority of God's standards because it can't. —Romans 8:7 GW

The unredeemed sinner may have a genuine inner desire to obey God but finds obedience to be unachievable (see Romans 7:19). Inwardly there is still a sinner, and until this sinful nature is crucified and buried with Christ, the dead spirit cannot be raised up with Christ into a new man whose nature is no longer sinful (see Romans 6:3–7; Ephesians 2:1). Only in this way can you or anyone else come to the end of disobedience and be saved.

- Why is it that your most natural state will always tend to want to show itself?
- What do you make of Hopeful's arguments about the causes of backsliding?
- How does the transformation of your mind help your walk with God?

Father, help me to cling to Your grace and live according to my new nature in Christ. May my life be fully surrendered to You by a complete and steadfast change of mind. Abandoning hope in myself, I look to Christ's cross, His grave and His empty tomb for the end of disobedience.

*In this land also, the contract between the bride
and the bridegroom was renewed.*

The Bible begins with a marriage after God declares that it is not good for the man to be alone. God fashioned Eve and presented her to Adam, and it was the end of singleness for him. The Bible ends with a marriage of the Church as the Bride to her Bridegroom, Christ.

Christian and Hopeful now pass into what seems like another world altogether. The air is no longer drowsy but fresh and sweet. Menacing characters dare not venture here, in plain sight of Celestial City, with the sun shining both day and night and the Shining Ones walking there often. This is sweet Beulah Land, *beulah* meaning "married."

> It will no longer be said to you, "Forsaken," nor to your land will it any longer be said, "Desolate"; but you will be called, "My delight is in her," and your land, "Married"; for the Lord delights in you, and to Him your land will be married. —Isaiah 62:4 NASB

The Bible contains a promise from God to be married to the land of Israel and to delight Himself in her. Since the establishment of the modern state of Israel in 1948, the land has turned from being mostly uncultivated to being a wonder of agricultural science.

God's "marrying" the land of Israel is an illustration of what will happen when you as a believer recognize and walk in your betrothal to Christ. Areas of your life that were previously unproductive will begin to flourish in miraculous ways. You will be blessed to be a blessing (see Genesis 12:2). Best of all, Christ will be with you every moment through His indwelling Spirit. Whatever your earthly relationship status is, you will know the end of singleness.

- Why did God consider it not good for Adam to be alone?
- How have you struggled with loneliness or questioning God's presence with you?
- What examples can you point to of how God's presence has brought fruitfulness?

Father, thank You that Christ instituted the Church to be like the ark, where I can get on board with other believers for mutual encouragement and be in fellowship. Thank You for the Holy Spirit, who lives inside to comfort, teach, guide and assure that I am never alone.

85 | THE END OF HELPLESSNESS

Two men met them there, in clothing that shone bright as gold.

Have you ever been through a period of such great trial that you began to despair and lose hope? Consider those who have endured wars, living as refugees, persecution, discrimination, homelessness or long-term sickness or disability. But then, by God's grace, there came a turning point when help arrived and with it the end of helplessness.

The two pilgrims meet the gardener of Beulah Land, who tells them the King has arranged these lands for His own delight and for the enjoyment and refreshment of pilgrims like them. Christian and Hopeful enjoy the fruits of the place, and then speak sweetly in their sleep. In the morning they journey on toward Celestial City and are met by two shining men sent to help pilgrims like them! It is the end of helplessness.

> They said to her, "You are out of your mind!" But she kept insisting that it was so. They said, "It is his angel." —Acts 12:15 NASB

We can become so used to living with hardship that we fail to believe it when help arrives. Rhoda was a servant in

Jerusalem at a house where fervent prayers were being made for the release of the apostle Peter from prison and his expected public execution. The angel of the Lord released Peter, and he arrived outside the prayer meeting. Rhoda left Peter waiting outside and ran to tell those inside that she had heard his voice outside the door. The reaction from inside was one of, "No, it can't be!"

Let us not be so hardened to the belief that our prayers have been answered, but rather let us be those who shout a praise when God brings us to the end of helplessness.

- When has God helped you when you have felt hopeless?
- How has the presence of God's "shining ones" strengthened you on your journey?
- How will you avoid being full of doubt when God grants you a miracle?

Father, through many dangers, toils and snares I have already come by Your grace, and by Your mercies I shall endure to the end and be saved. Thank You for Your miraculous provision in my life. Grant me greater faith and trust in You to believe and receive Your miracles. Send Your shining ones to help me and dispel all hopelessness.

Then they both took courage, and the enemy remained as still as a stone, until they had crossed over.

The death of a believer, when approached consciously, is a trying time. There are those of strong faith who openly speak of how they long to cross from this world to the next, but they are the exception, not the rule. Studies confirm that there is a general tendency among older believers to become more earnest in their faith, knowing their days on earth are approaching an end. Stronger faith leads to less intimidation.

The two pilgrims are led to the river by the Shining Ones and are told they must each cross it alone. They become despondent, but being told there is no other way, they start across. Christian finds it hardest, as he thinks of his failings in life. But Hopeful is his true friend and encourager, until Christian encounters Christ through the eyes and ears of faith, and, discovering the end of intimidation, they cross safely over.

When you pass through the waters, I will be with you; and through the rivers, they will not overflow you. When you walk through the fire, you will not be scorched, nor will the flame burn you. —Isaiah 43:2 NASB

One can but wonder how many of the Holocaust victims thought of these words when they entered the extermination camps in Europe. The guards would taunt them, saying, "You came in through the gates, but you will exit via the chimney."

The devil seeks to create doubt and fear in your heart and mind when you face danger or death. During such moments of trial, we need to remember and act on the words of Christ, who instructs us to "take courage; I have overcome the world" (John 16:33). To do so is the end of intimidation.

- How have you overcome intimidation?
- How are you consciously preparing yourself to meet Jesus?
- How can you increase your assurance of Christ's declaration of victory?

Father, may I take account of myself and purposefully invest more of my time and attention into preparing myself to cross the river into eternal life. May I take hold of Christ's many promises toward me and work with them to build confidence in the truth and power of His Word.

What's more, when he shall again return to the city, you shall go too, with a trumpet sound, and be with him forever.

From Paradise (see Luke 23:43) the waiting saints who have died in Christ shall be gathered and rise with the Lord, to be joined by the saints on earth in the air, and then the gathered dead and living saints shall always be with the Lord (see 1 Thessalonians 4:16–17). What a glorious day!

Having crossed the river, the two pilgrims leave their mortal clothes behind and are met by the Shining Ones, who escort them to the gate of the Celestial City. There they are greeted with a loud and joyful welcome. They are about to be clothed in a glorious new way, signaling the end of death.

> For the Lord Himself will descend from heaven with a shout, with the voice of the archangel and with the trumpet of God, and the dead in Christ will rise first. —1 Thessalonians 4:16 NASB

The death of Christ occurred alongside the resurrection of many dead saints in Jerusalem (see Matthew 27:52). The penalty of sin had been paid in full, and these saints rose together with Christ as part of the firstfruits of that great act of redemption (see 1 Corinthians 15:20). Believers since then will be part of a great harvest of souls of all those who have heard, believed and responded rightly to the gospel of Christ as Lord and Savior.

Even the wicked will be raised, but only to face judgment and punishment (see Revelation 20:11–15). As a believer, you can look forward with certainty to the resurrection and be assured of a wonderful eternity in the presence of Christ and the saints. You will see the end of death when it is cast with hell into the lake of fire (see Revelation 20:14).

- Who do you most look forward to seeing at the resurrection of the saints?
- In what ways do the death and resurrection of Christ give you a sure hope?
- What excites you most about heaven?

Father, help me not to become so comfortable on earth that I don't look forward to a new heaven and earth! Thank You that because Christ rose from the dead and is alive today, I have a sure and certain hope. I am so excited that I will see You face to face.

88 | THE END OF OUR PILGRIMAGE

Then each of the Pilgrims gave to them individually his certificate,
which they had received when they started out;
and those were brought to the King.

Each of us ought to make sure of our own salvation, not by our own good deeds, but rather by trust in the atoning work of the cross of Christ, and the subsequent transforming work of the Holy Spirit in our lives, which leads us to godliness and demonstration of Christ's life in us.

The pilgrims present their carefully guarded certificates to the gatekeepers, who send them on to the King. The King personally checks them and inquires where the men are. Being told they are outside the gate, the King commands that they be brought in. As the pilgrims enter, they are clothed with what looks like shining gold. Praises resound all around, and the pilgrims join in the joyful song of praise to God and the Lamb.

> Nothing unclean, and no one who practices abomination and lying, shall ever come into it, but only those whose names are written in the Lamb's book of life. —Revelation 21:27 NASB

Like Christian and Hopeful, we must persevere and press through, enduring countless dangers and trials, until we at last reach heaven itself. That was the end of their pilgrimage, and it is also the end of ours.

How can you be sure your name is written in the Lamb's Book of Life? You must ensure that you have sincerely repented of your sins, turned to Christ for salvation, and trusted that He paid the price for your sins, and be diligently following Him and the leading of His Holy Spirit (see Ephesians 1:10–14). Do these things, and you can be sure of reaching the end of your pilgrimage.

- How are you making sure of your own salvation?
- What do you think the King might have read on the certificates presented to Him?
- What comes to mind when you consider reaching the end of your pilgrimage?

Father, Your Word tells me to make my calling and choosing sure. I am sure that You have called me; help me to make sure that what I choose aligns with Your will for my life. When I consider the joys that await the saints, may I seek Your face more. I want to hear the words, "Well done, good and faithful servant."

Behold, the City shone like the sun; the streets also were
paved with gold, and in them walked many men,
with crowns on their heads.

Entry to heaven as a citizen means the end of sadness. Heaven's citizens shall live in an earth where justice rolls like a river and righteousness like a constant stream (see Amos 5:24). Their King shall sit in the new Jerusalem upon David's throne, be the greatest King ever and reign forever and ever (see Isaiah 9:7). His throne and the throne of God Himself shall be beside each other (see Hebrews 12:2; Revelation 22:3).

Looking inside the Celestial City, the dreamer sees many people walking and wearing golden crowns, some waving palm branches and others playing golden harps, while they all sing praises. He also sees some winged creatures who cry out continually, "Holy, holy, holy is the Lord." It is such a joyous and vibrant scene that the dreamer wishes he were present there among them.

> And the street of the city was pure gold, like transparent glass.
> —Revelation 21:21 NASB

Many songwriters have written eloquently of the beauty of the heaven that Christ has been preparing the past 2,000 years (see John 14:3), yet to behold its glorious beauty and splendor will surely make even the most eloquent descriptions seem vastly inadequate.

It will not be possible for you to be sad in heaven, for God Himself will wipe every tear from the eyes of His precious saints. Death and sickness will be no more. There will be a new earth and a new Jerusalem on earth that comes down from heaven, and God will move in (see Revelation 21:1–3)! Life in the presence of God and the Lamb will bring the end of sadness.

- What distinctives of heaven are you most looking forward to?
- What creates sadness on earth that will no longer be present in heaven?
- How might you feel wearing your crown and walking on the streets of heaven?

Father, parts of this present earth are breathtakingly beautiful and cause my soul to praise You. How much more shall joy and gladness fill my heart when I am forever with You and Christ in eternity. Help me to endure the temporary light afflictions of earth knowing the glories of what lies ahead.

Then they asked him for his certificate, that they might go in and show it to the King; so he fumbled in his bosom for one, and found none.

Doing no homework and fooling around in classes may seem like a lot of fun at the time, but when the day of examination comes, there will surely be a reckoning. It may mean leaving with no graduation certificate and discovering that no employer is interested to give you work. But fooling around in life and failing to understand that there will be a final exam is far more serious (see Hebrews 9:27).

After his view into Celestial City closes, the dreamer sees Ignorance crossing the river with a ferryman called Vain-hope. Ignorance comes boldly to the gate, but when asked for his certificate, he is unable to produce one. Word reaches the King, who sends back orders that Ignorance should be bound and cast out into outer darkness. Such is the end of the wicked.

Then the king said to the servants, "Tie his hands and feet, and throw him into the outer darkness; there will be weeping and gnashing of teeth in that place." —Matthew 22:13 NASB

The King in this parable is God, who gave a wedding feast for His Son, Jesus, on the day of His marriage to His Bride, the Church. Someone thought he could just walk in uninvited and share the joy, the hospitality and the benefits of this great occasion. After all, the guests would eat freely from the tree of life (see Revelation 22:14). But the man stood out badly because his clothes looked like rags compared to the invited guests, and when he was asked to explain why, he could not, and he was thrown outside. Such is the end of the wicked.

- Examine yourself to find any areas in your life where you have been careless.
- Why will some be surprised to discover they are not going to be saved?
- How do you suppose Ignorance felt to be thrown out at the very gate?

Father, help me to carefully examine my life by the light of Your Word and the searching of Your Spirit. Show me every area that requires correction, and grant me grace to repent and make right, that I may be counted worthy of my calling and enter into Your joy.

Special Invitation

Dear Reader,

You have reached the end of this devotional and possibly have also finished reading *Pilgrim's Progress*. You may have observed how difficult it is to attain to life in the Celestial City, but also how easy. It is impossible to reach there on your own merit, but equally it is entirely possible to reach there with a childlike faith. That faith must rest wholly on what Christ did in dying for sinners on the cross of Calvary.

Christ died for you. Do you believe this? If so, invite Him to wash you thoroughly from your sins. His literal blood was shed all those years ago, but you see it, take it and apply it to your dead and sinful life by faith. When you do so, your dead soul will be born again, not like a human baby but as a child of heaven, born of Christ's blood and confirmed by baptism in water and by His Spirit.

This is the starting point of your pilgrimage, and it can be every bit as exciting, rewarding and sure as that of Christian and Hopeful. If you are ready to begin, you may do so by praying this prayer and truly meaning every word.